ALSO BY RIAD SATTOUF

The Arab of the Future, Volume 1:
A Childhood in the Middle East, 1978–1984

The Arab of the Future, Volume 2:
A Childhood in the Middle East, 1984–1985

THE ARAB
OF THE FUTURE 3

A GRAPHIC MEMOIR

A Childhood in the Middle East (1985–1987)

RIAD SATTOUF

TRANSLATED BY SAM TAYLOR

METROPOLITAN BOOKS   HENRY HOLT AND COMPANY   NEW YORK

Metropolitan Books
Henry Holt and Company
Publishers since 1866
175 Fifth Avenue
New York, New York 10010

Metropolitan Books® and ® are registered trademarks of
Macmillan Publishing Group, LLC.

Originally published in France in 2016 by Allary Éditions

Library of Congress Cataloging-in-Publication data for the first volume is as follow:

Sattouf, Riad, author.
  [Arabe du futur. English]
  The Arab of the future : growing up in the Middle East (1978–1984) : a graphic memoir / Riad Sattouf ;
translated from the French by Sam Taylor.
     pages cm
  ISBN 978-1-62779-344-5 (hardback)—ISBN (invalid) 978-1-62779-345-2 (electronic book)
1. Sattouf, Riad—Childhood and youth—Comic books, strips, etc. 2. Cartoonists—France—Biography—
Comic books, strips, etc. 3. Middle East—Biography—Comic books, strips, etc. 4. Graphic novels.
I. Taylor, Sam, 1970– translator. II. Title.
  NC1499.S337A2 2015
  741.5'69092–dc23
  [B]   2014041152

ISBN: 978-1-62779-353-7

Our books may be purchased in bulk for promotional, educational, or business use. Please contact your
local bookseller or the Macmillan Corporate and Premium Sales Department at (800) 221-7945, extension
5442, or by e-mail at MacmillanSpecialMarkets@macmillan.com.

First U.S. Edition 2018

Designed by Kelly S. Too
Typography and composition by Jonathan Bennett
The author would like to thank Charline Bailot for her help.

Printed in China
10 9 8 7 6 5 4 3 2 1

CHAPTER 1

My name is Riad. In 1985, I was seven years old and I was amazing.

Wavy dark-blond hair

Smell of chamomile shampoo from France

My sixth cardboard book bag

Looks a bit smug

Very neat and tidy

Scrawny from too many stomach bugs

I still lived in Ter Maaleh in Syria, with my parents and my little brother.

The house was unchanged on the outside

Inside, the walls had been painted pale blue and my mother had hung pictures in the living room.

She'd finished the big tapestry

It took me three years and now here it is.

My father sometimes wore glasses.

He still taught a few classes every week in Damascus

These glasses are just to rest my eyes. I can see perfectly well without them.

My eyesight is excellent.

He looked a bit older

THE TAP WATER IS BROWN!

WHAT ARE THE KIDS SUPPOSED TO DRINK?

I'M SICK OF THIS!

My mother often got mad at my father because of our living conditions.

What can I do? I'll buy bottled water!

I painted the walls! I hung pictures! In France, you wouldn't have a house as nice as this!

I'm sick of this! I want to live in a city!

We can't bring up children like this!

I WANT A CAR!

A CAR?!? YOU KNOW HOW MUCH A MERCEDES COSTS?

I DON'T CARE IF IT'S A MERCEDES. BUY A PEUGEOT!

A FRENCH CAR?!? NEVER!

All I need is two good harvests and we can build the villa!

NO!

I want to live in a city! DAMASCUS! ALEPPO! Or at least HOMS! I can't stand it here anymore!

There are power cuts all the time, the kids are always sick . . .

Sniff

Well, I wanted this to be a surprise, but if you insist, I'll tell you now. I've made friends with a very important person.

Really?

He's close to President Assad. He's going to help me become a full professor, so I can earn more money.

Who is it?

It's a secret.

We'll get an invitation soon, just wait! You'll see the powerful connections I've made.

You just need to be A LITTLE PATIENT.

You French women, you always want everything right away.

Syrian women don't question their husbands.

They do what they're told and that's it.

My father was always trying to show his power over my mother. But he was scared of her.

We'll visit Damascus with my friend!

About time! I haven't left this hole in three years!

And I don't want to visit, I want to LIVE THERE.

But ... what about our vacation in Latakia? The Meridien Hotel?

Give me a break! We never hear from the general, and he only lives 200 yards away!

And I keep seeing your ex-brother-in-law the murderer walking past the window, and I'm afraid!

When my parents argued, I went to our bedroom.

My brother, Yahya, seemed completely unaware of all this.

VVVVVRRROOOM!!!! TOOT TOOT!

CLANG

My favorite thing in the world was taunting him.

HEY! DON'T TOUCH MY TOYS, YOU LITTLE FREAK!

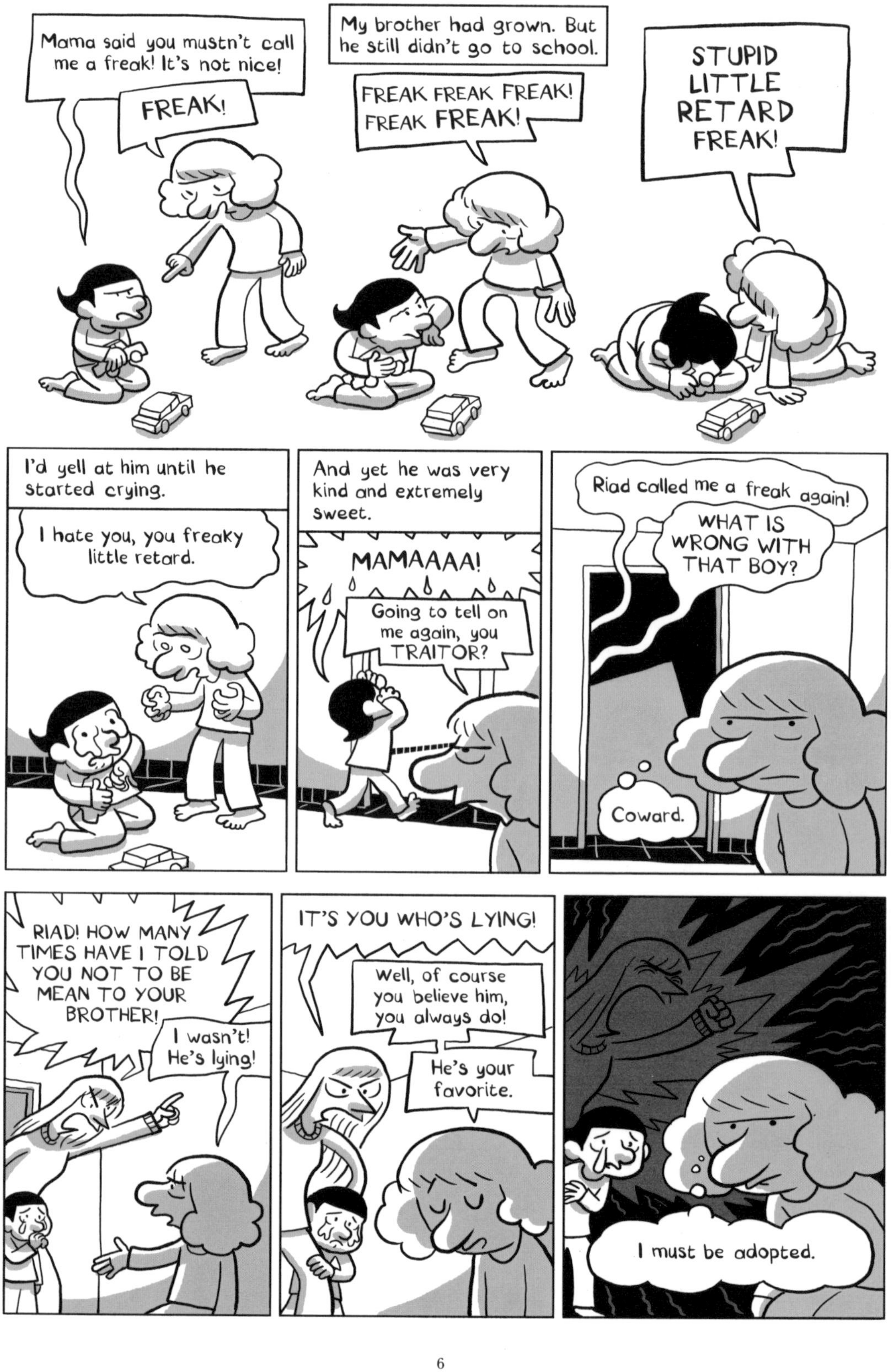

Mama said you mustn't call me a freak! It's not nice!
FREAK!
My brother had grown. But he still didn't go to school.
FREAK FREAK FREAK! FREAK FREAK!
STUPID LITTLE RETARD FREAK!
I'd yell at him until he started crying.
I hate you, you freaky little retard.
And yet he was very kind and extremely sweet.
MAMAAAA!
Going to tell on me again, you TRAITOR?
Riad called me a freak again!
WHAT IS WRONG WITH THAT BOY?
Coward.
RIAD! HOW MANY TIMES HAVE I TOLD YOU NOT TO BE MEAN TO YOUR BROTHER!
I wasn't! He's lying!
IT'S YOU WHO'S LYING!
Well, of course you believe him, you always do!
He's your favorite.
I must be adopted.

I was coming to the end of my third year at the village school. It had moved to a new building and was for boys only.

Cracks in the new concrete

My father's field was over here

No toilets

Pile of cement

It smelled of urine and pine trees

Gate without a fence

The girls went to the old school, next door.

I saw them walk by in the distance

Like all the boys, I had no contact with them. And I wasn't interested.

I was still friends with Saleem

When we sang the national anthem in the morning, we were now accompanied by a boom box at top volume.

DEFENDERS OF OUR HOMELAND, PEACE BE WITH YOU! OUR NOBLE SPIRITS WILL NOT BE SUBDUED!

I tried to sing louder than the others

I was the best in my class, as my father expected me to be.

Saleem was a good student, too. We always sat together in the front row.

No one wanted to sit next to us

Our teacher looked like James Dean with a mustache, and we idolized him.

Take out your homework. I'm going to check it.

QUICK!

Everyone look at Riad and Saleem! Sitting there quietly with their homework out, before I even had to ask, waiting for me to check it.

I'm not even going to bother checking their work. There's no point.

I'm sure it's perfect.

Disappointed not to get praise

The other children had been toughened up by their beatings. They didn't like us. At all.

They glared at us. We had to avoid meeting their eyes

Who hasn't done his homework? If you confess, I'll only hit you once.

Only two? LAST CHANCE. If I find someone who hasn't done his homework and hasn't confessed, he's DEAD.

I hadn't been beaten in a long time. It was easy—I just did everything the teacher told me to.

WHAT? YOU DIDN'T DO YOUR HOMEWORK AND YOU DIDN'T OWN UP?

DOG! CRACK!
DOG! CRACK!
DOG! CRACK!
DOG! CRACK!
CRACKK

YOU DOG! YOUR STUPID HEAD BROKE MY CANE!

Waah

I didn't understand why anyone would disobey the teacher. Doing what he said was a lot less painful than not doing it.

PLEASE, FOR THE LOVE OF GOD, HAVE MERCY!

Pfft

All of you listen! My cane is broken! So on Saturday I want you each to bring me a new cane.

I will choose the one that's hardest and most effective...

...and that will be my new cane.

We hung out near the teachers at recess because there were always fights going on.

We stared at our feet to avoid looking at the other boys

Thirty students played soccer with the same ball.

Heads shaved because of lice

But sometimes, despite our efforts, one of the boys caught us looking at them.

?

When the teacher had gone, they'd shout at me.

Psst, Frenchy! You looking at me?

Speak French right now or I'll kill you!

Bien sur!

CHABADI-RABADI ZEU-ZEU BADA CHABAZI LA LA RHEUFEUFEU!

HA HA HA! BA HA HA

He's speaking French! It sounds like puking!

CHABADI RABADI!

Go on, beat it!

Hhh Hhh

I knew what I had to do to survive.

10

My father was proud of my grades. I had an average of 10/10.

It's good, it's good, but the problem with 10/10 is that you can't improve . . .

You can only get worse . . .

SCRATCH
SCRATCH

No, but it's good. Keep going. Don't pay any attention to the other boys and always obey your teacher.

People hate anyone who's better than them. Never forget that.

If you're top of the class, that means you're smarter and better than the others.

And that means you have to watch out.

Because one day, the others will get sick of you always beating them.

They may be stupid, but there are MORE OF THEM.

They'll gang up AGAINST YOU.

That's what is known as the TRIUMPH OF THE DUMBEST.

So always be modest and reserved. Crush them, but do it quietly. And be charitable.

Hmm. The problem is that it's hard to be modest when you're so much better than all those morons . . .

But . . . well, that's how life is for the son of a great man like me.

HA HA HA HA

Anyway, well done. Keep it up.

Don't let your grades drop!

We still visited my grandmother regularly.

Aaah ... I feel weak. I don't think I'm long for this world ...

My mother didn't know Arabic, so she didn't realize that my grandmother constantly scolded my father about religion.

... You don't pray, you don't go to the mosque, you act like you're European ...

No, you don't understand. I'm modern! I'm a modern Muslim!

Oh, I pray that you're telling the truth ...

... because I've had a hard life, I've lost two children, and now I'm old, and when I die I'll stand before God and he'll say to me, "Why is your son Abdel-Razak an unbeliever?"

And I'll say, "He's modern, forgive him! Look at my other children—they are all true believers ..."

But he'll say, "NO, he's not modern, he's an infidel who abandoned his faith!"

And you know what God will say then? "Your duty as a mother was to raise a true believer! How dare you pretend to worship me all these years? YOU RAISED AN INFIDEL, THAT'S WHAT YOU DID!"

"So now I'm going to take your modern son to heaven, and I'm going to send you to HELL!"

ACCHHH!

Is that what you want for your poor old mother? After a life of poverty, the fires of hell?

NOOO ... PFFFT

12

Personally, I had grave doubts about the existence of God. I just couldn't make myself believe.

Ahhh! My darlings!

Come! Come!

So I pretended, thinking that maybe faith would come one day.

Hello, my uncle.

Hello, Anas!

In my family, they spent their time talking about God and invoking his name.

Hadj Mohamed, my brother!

They praised the qualities of moral purity, honesty, kindness, sincerity ... and showed none of them.

So, Riad! When are you going to let Anas and Moktar play with your toys?

The way they behaved was the exact opposite of the things they said.

Yes! You could ask them over to play for once!

It seemed obvious to me that if God existed, he would not allow such hypocrisy.

Yeah that's true, we want to come over!

And play with your toys!

The fact that he never intervened to punish their spitefulness could mean only one thing.

CRAK

He did not exist.

There were only two supernatural phenomena that I knew were real.

Yank it hard, it'll come out.

The first was the mysterious "little mouse."

Just put your tooth under your pillow tonight, and the little mouse will come, and leave you a coin in its place!

I was losing my milk teeth

And the next morning, there really was a one-pound coin where my tooth had been!

AMAZING!

Each time, I tried to stay awake as long as possible so I could see the mouse ...

... but the little mouse was very smart and always waited until I was asleep

As I was obsessed by animals, I kept asking my father about this mysterious type of mouse.

They're bigger and smarter than normal mice. They live all over the world and collect children's teeth! They're very special.

Of course we have them in Syria. They're Syrian mice. They collect teeth, too. They speak Arabic and are just as smart as the others.

Marvelous teeth!

I tried to catch them in the act, but I never could.

One time I ALMOST did. But it ran away from me!

The second supernatural phenomenon that I knew about was, of course, Santa Claus.

HE'LL BE HERE SOON! HAVE YOU BEEN GOOD?

YES, MAMA

Santa Claus was a magical old man with a white beard, dressed in red, who watched our behavior all year round.

He lived in the sky

You never saw his eyes

Quite well behaved, that Riad ...

You had to write him a list of your dream gifts ...

Dear Santa, this is what I would like:
- a Big Jim helicopter
- a Big Jim spaceship
- a real pistol with real bullets
Thank you, Riad!

Your parents mailed the letter ...

They really did mail it

Then you put up a tree and decorated it with shiny baubles and strings of lights ...

And you sprayed the tree with fake snow, which had a synthetic smell

Paper bag

You went to bed ...

Fall asleep quick! Quick quick quick!

... and in the morning, you rushed downstairs to find the presents Santa left under the tree in the night!

This was proof that magic really existed.

The box for the Big Jim helicopter looks kind of small ...

Santa had only ever come when we were in France ...

A Big Jim diver? Doesn't Santa know French?

... never in Syria.

This year I want a proper Christmas, like in France!

I'M SICK OF THIS!

Take it easy! You don't need to yell!

I'll do what I can, ok?

My father took us shopping in Homs.

I want foie gras, champagne, and a Christmas tree!

HOW DO YOU EXPECT ME TO FIND A CHRISTMAS TREE IN HOMS?

Ha ha, just kidding! We'll make it a real celebration! I'm going to buy a bottle of Côtes du Rhône, my favorite wine.

Homs hadn't changed. The streets were still jammed with traffic.

The grocery stores were almost empty. They only sold one or two items . . .

Let's buy some Chiclets from this poor kid. They're like gum, but even better!

One pound, sir!

Mmm, a delicious minty flavor! I feel bad for that kid. Let's be kind and give him one.

A true believer is always charitable.

Here, my child, have a Chiclet.

No thanks, I don't like the taste.

He's living on the street and he doesn't like Chiclets! Now I've seen it all!

See what I mean about the triumph of the dumbest?

My father took us to a store we'd never seen before.

Clean windows, not like the others

Doorbell

He rang the bell. A guy in a suit opened the door.

Hello, I'd like to buy some champagne.

Of course, sir. Come in.

The guy went back behind his counter.

Don't hesitate to ask if you have any questions.

Very clean floor

The store was full of expensive wines displayed in little wall alcoves.

All the prices were in dollars.

Ohhh! Foie gras! I want some! With white bread!

My father had brought an envelope full of bills and he looked inside it whenever my mother said she wanted something.

Ohhhhhhhh! Caviar!

Go ahead honey, take it . . .

There was a toy corner with boxes of Legos.

They looked like treasure in that light

Suddenly, I sensed a presence above me.

I looked up and was blown away by the most beautiful thing I had ever seen in my life!

17

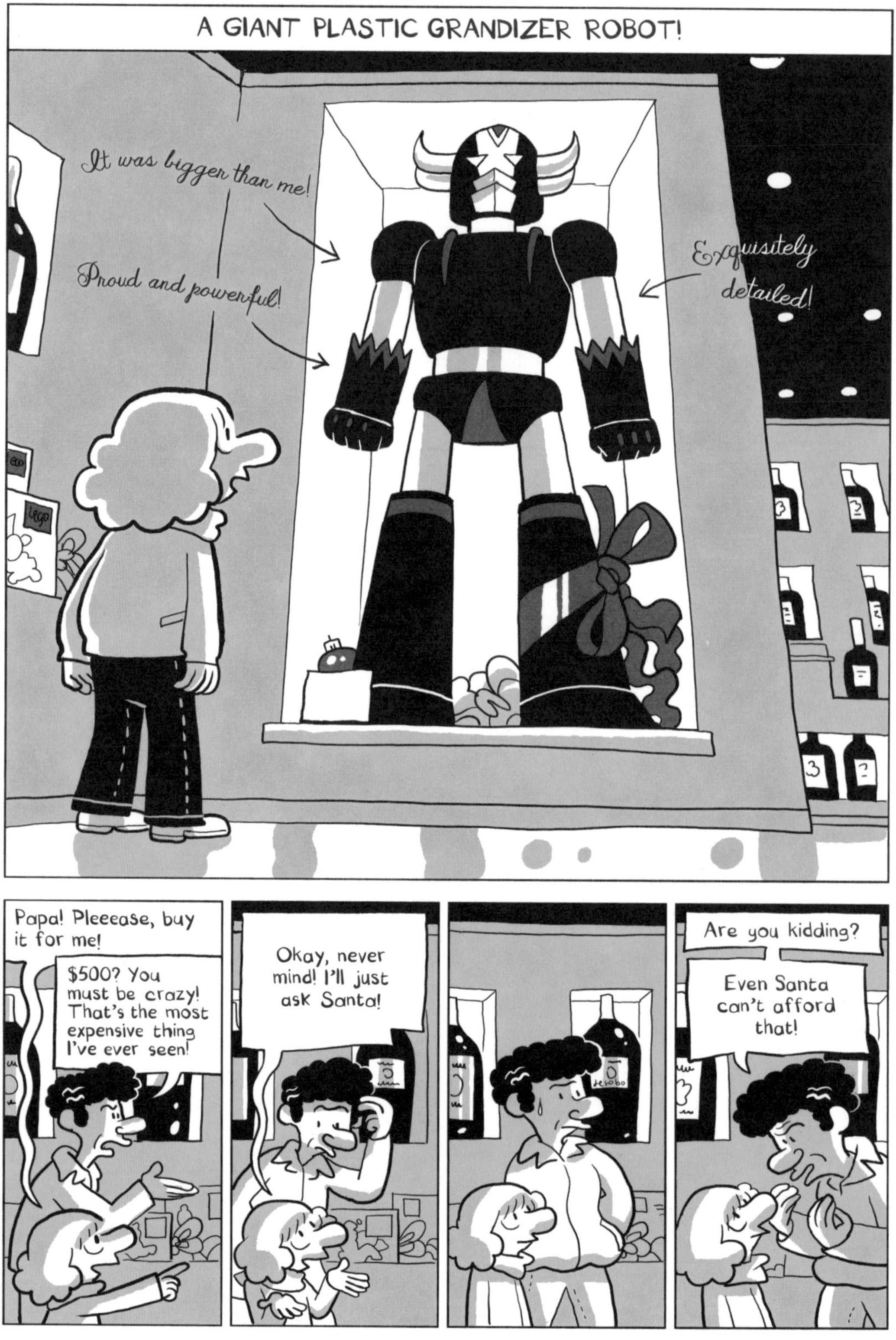
A GIANT PLASTIC GRANDIZER ROBOT!
It was bigger than me!
Proud and powerful!
Exquisitely detailed!
Papa! Pleeease, buy it for me!
$500? You must be crazy! That's the most expensive thing I've ever seen!
Okay, never mind! I'll just ask Santa!
Are you kidding?
Even Santa can't afford that!

At that moment, a huge Mercedes stopped outside the store.

Mercedes Sonderklasse W126, that's luxury!

It had a foreign license plate.

A small, anxious man got out of the car and rang the bell.

Hello, sir.

Huff Huff Huff Huff

He asked for three bottles of the most expensive wine.

Vosne-Romanée, $1,000.

That's really the most expensive one?

Yes, sir.

He paid, put the bottles in the trunk, and got back behind the wheel.

CLAC!

HONK HONK HONK

VRROAR

I asked my father where the license plate was from.

It's Saudi . . . But the guy we saw was just their Filipino.

He was scared that if he took the wrong bottle back to his master, he'd be beaten to death with it.

That's what they're like in Saudi Arabia!

What's Saudi Arabia?

WHOO HOO!

Saudi Arabia is where Mecca is, the holiest place in the Islamic world! It's a very tough country, but everyone there is rich.

The capital has a nice name: Riyadh!

LIKE YOU!

It means God's garden!

The country was created by a VERY smart warlord called Al-Saud. It was named after him—can you imagine?

It's like I founded a country and called it Sattoufi Arabia!

Before the Al-Sauds, it was a desert with Bedouin tribes fighting each other all the time... Real desert vagrants...

They were dumb, ignorant bigots, so Al-Saud killed them all and said, "I'm in charge." But no one cared about his country until they discovered oil there. And not just a drop: an OCEAN of it. That was in 1936.

You can even find oil there in the streets.

So after that, of course, the Americans became their best friends and showered them with dollars in return for oil to run their big cars ...

And within a few years, the Saudi leaders were billionaires ...

But the people were mad at the leaders for their immoral behavior and because they were friends with the Americans, who support Israel ...

But the leaders acted like everything was fine.

And in 1979, the year after you were born, something terrible happened! Some hostages were taken in Mecca ...

... by ISLAMISTS!

They were young fanatics. They surrounded the Kaaba and declared that the Al-Sauds had lost the right to rule over Islam's holiest place because they were corrupted by American Jews and infidels.

THEY WEREN'T WRONG, HA HA, but what do you expect?

There's nothing better than dollars.

France sent troops to help the Saudis and the siege was ended.

REALLY? FRANCE? How come?

Yes, France! They buy oil from the Sauds, too!

For their ugly little Citroëns, ha ha ha!

So, thanks to the French, the hostage takers were arrested . . . and the Saudis beheaded them live on television.

They cut off their heads with sabers, like the ones on that car's license plate . . .

. . . AS A WARNING!

After that, the Saudi government made lots of strict religious laws to control people, and now it's a harsh Islamic nation.

Women have very few rights, and the whole society is based on the Quran . . . And why not? That's life in a Muslim country.

But if you claim to be the truest believers in the world, why send your slave to buy alcohol?

THAT'S THE SAUDIS FOR YOU!

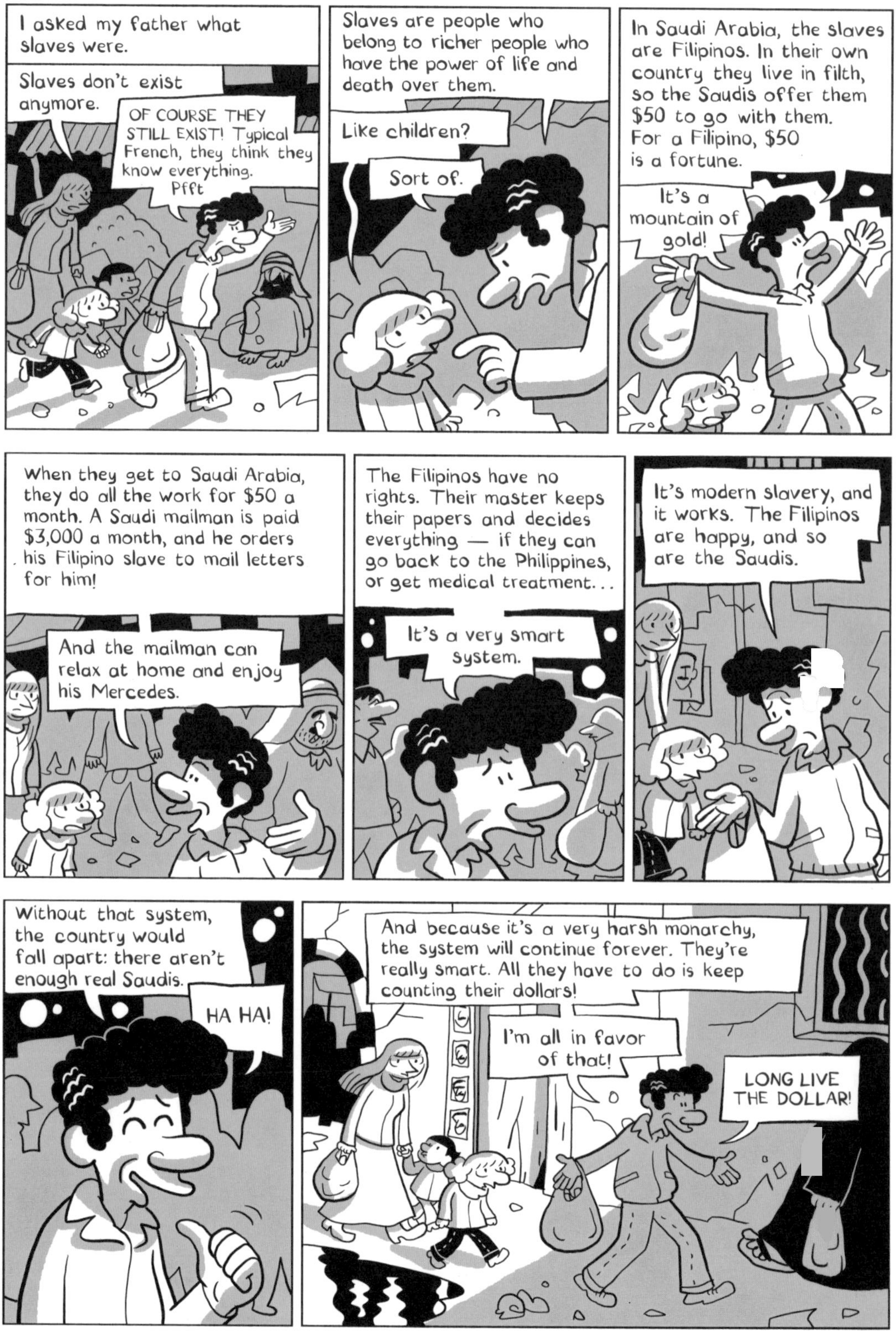
I asked my father what slaves were.
Slaves don't exist anymore.
OF COURSE THEY STILL EXIST! Typical French, they think they know everything. Pfft
Slaves are people who belong to richer people who have the power of life and death over them.
Like children?
Sort of.
In Saudi Arabia, the slaves are Filipinos. In their own country they live in filth, so the Saudis offer them $50 to go with them. For a Filipino, $50 is a fortune.
It's a mountain of gold!
When they get to Saudi Arabia, they do all the work for $50 a month. A Saudi mailman is paid $3,000 a month, and he orders his Filipino slave to mail letters for him!
And the mailman can relax at home and enjoy his Mercedes.
The Filipinos have no rights. Their master keeps their papers and decides everything — if they can go back to the Philippines, or get medical treatment...
It's a very smart system.
It's modern slavery, and it works. The Filipinos are happy, and so are the Saudis.
Without that system, the country would fall apart: there aren't enough real Saudis.
HA HA!
And because it's a very harsh monarchy, the system will continue forever. They're really smart. All they have to do is keep counting their dollars!
I'm all in favor of that!
LONG LIVE THE DOLLAR!

How can you approve of such an awful country? I read in *Paris Match* that women have to stay at home. They aren't allowed to go out alone, that and they have to wear black veils.

I don't "approve" of it. You and your fancy words!

But it's an Islamic nation. That's how it is. It's Muslim tradition. It's normal for true believers to live like that.

It's not so different from life in the village, just a bit stricter . . . But with dollars!

Life is always better with dollars!

I tell you what, if you said to the French, "We're going to get rid of freedom of speech, human rights, and democracy, and pay everyone $3,000 for doing nothing and give free healthcare . . . What do you think?" I tell you, the French would say . . .

"Where do I sign? Can I get my dollars today?"

No one would care about all your big ideas!

The whole world wants dollars. That's why America is so powerful.

One day, all those terrible Gulf countries will buy everything in France. Even people's hearts. You'll see. And the French will grin like idiots and thank them . . .

THANK YOU! THANK YOU FOR THE NICE DOLLARS!

But anyway. It's true that the Saudis are scum.

I went there in 1943. I remember it vividly.

REALLY?

Oh yeah, I was young, but I remember it well.

I was three or four. It was just after my father died. My mother wanted to make her pilgrimage so we set off on foot to Tartus.

People were happy to let us stay with them when they found out we were on our pilgrimage . . . I was happy because I had my mother all to myself.

She was a young widow, and she was afraid she might die soon too. And because she'd lost two boys before me, she was afraid I would die. She didn't want us to die before we'd been to Mecca.

Why did the two boys die?

No one knew. They were babies. They were fine when they went to sleep, but in the morning they were cold and dead.

Good night!

Goo!

It was all so sad!

My poor brothers!

Anyway, we eventually got to Tartus. It seemed vast to peasants like us! We got lost.

But we ended up finding a huge ship. My mother paid a lot of money and we went into the hold with all these other people. . .

KARABUDJAN

. . . and we sat there. The ship was rocking and people were throwing up and it smelled really bad, but I was with my mother so I was happy.

We went through the Suez Canal and it was beautiful. There were big ships everywhere. I'd never seen anything like it.

At last we arrived in Jeddah, the big port near Mecca.

We made our pilgrimage and my mother wept when we walked around the Kaaba.

But there were so many people that I lost my mother in the crowd! I was crying, and all I could see were legs!

The worst day of my life!

I was calling out MAMA! MAMA! I thought I'd lost her forever!

MAMA!
MAMA!

He was shouting in the street

And then ... a MIRACLE! I bumped into someone, and it was her! That proves there is a God!

PAF

Then a Saudi rushed up to us and started beating us with a stick because we were circling the Kaaba the wrong way!

What kind of beast attacks a woman and her child? No animal would do that! SON OF A DOG!

Your grandmother couldn't move her arm afterward, and I was covered in bruises and had a terrible headache ... But we'd made our pilgrimage, so we were happy.

All these stories... they're so violent!

TERRIBLY VIOLENT!

Life was cheap back then. People died like that!

Life is better now!

We can eat foie gras and drink champagne like they do in France!

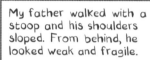

My father walked with a stoop and his shoulders sloped. From behind, he looked weak and fragile.

And yet, I felt sure that some great strength lay hidden inside him.

Papa! The store with the Grandizer, it was run by a Christian, wasn't it?

OBVIOUSLY! Who else would sell wine at ten times the normal price?

Suit-wearing Christian assholes!

26

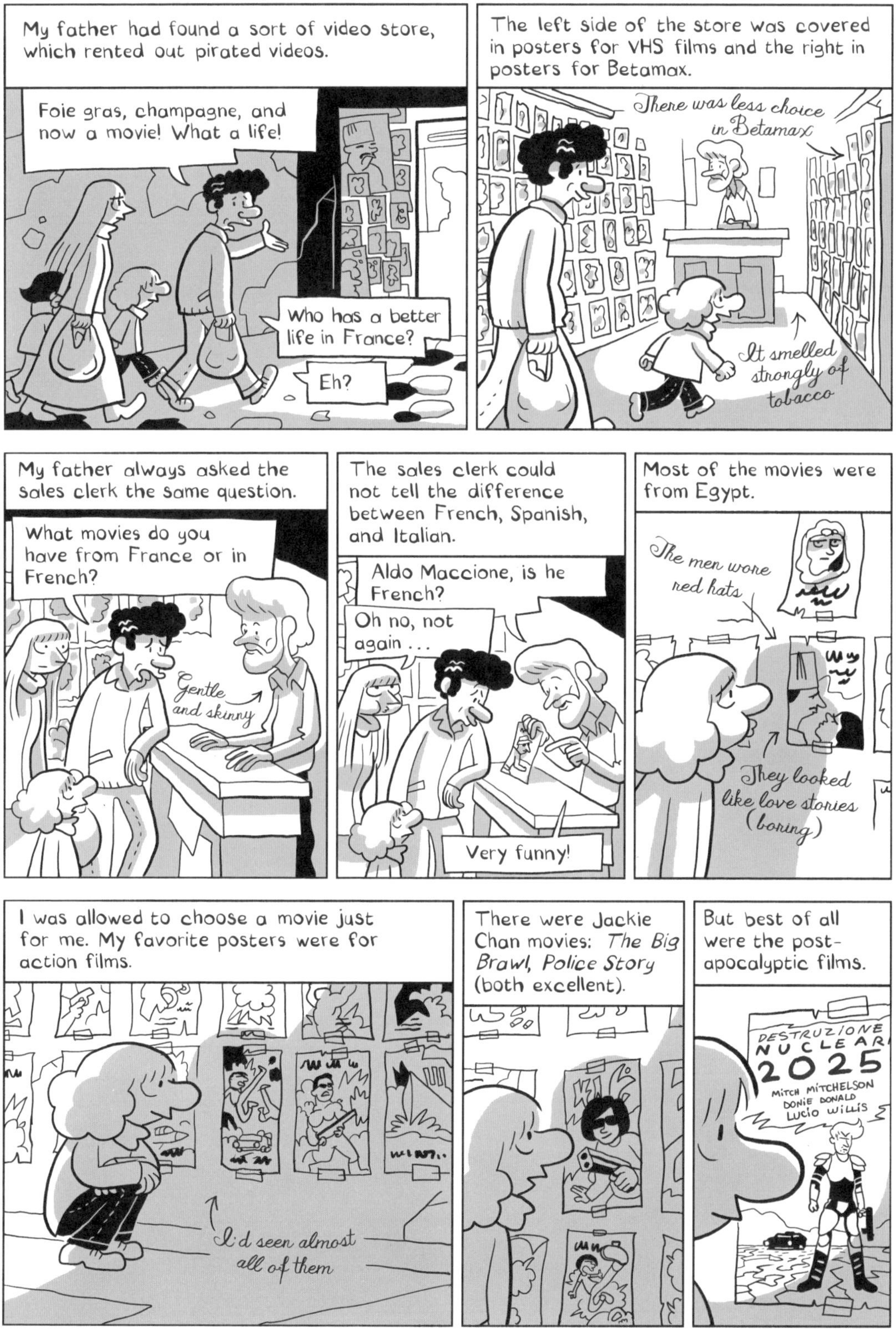

My father had found a sort of video store, which rented out pirated videos.
Foie gras, champagne, and now a movie! What a life!
Who has a better life in France?
Eh?
The left side of the store was covered in posters for VHS films and the right in posters for Betamax.
There was less choice in Betamax
It smelled strongly of tobacco
My father always asked the sales clerk the same question.
What movies do you have from France or in French?
Gentle and skinny
The sales clerk could not tell the difference between French, Spanish, and Italian.
Aldo Maccione, is he French?
Oh no, not again . . .
Very funny!
Most of the movies were from Egypt.
The men wore red hats
They looked like love stories (boring)
I was allowed to choose a movie just for me. My favorite posters were for action films.
I'd seen almost all of them
There were Jackie Chan movies: *The Big Brawl, Police Story* (both excellent).
But best of all were the post-apocalyptic films.
DESTRUZIONE NUCLEAR
2025
MITCH MITCHELSON
DONIE DONALD
LUCIO WILLIS

The story was always more or less the same.

Civilization had been wiped out by a nuclear war . . .

. . . but one man, alone, was struggling to survive

This warrior was usually an Italian beefcake with stylish hair, driving a powerful, beat-up car.

He was pursued by a pack . . .

Bastardi . . .

. . . of ultraviolent guys with Mohawks who wanted to kill him.

I loved those movies, and so did the sales clerk.

I've got something a little different that just came in.

Plenty of action and violence.

A masterpiece.

He showed me a photograph and said the name:

CONAN THE BARBARIAN

I'd never seen such a handsome, muscular man in my life. I was blown away.

I WANT IT.

Check with the guy that it's not too violent . . . There's a sword . . .

Swords are fine. It's sex that you have to watch out for.

Is it okay for a seven year old?

It's a man's film . . .

We'd been living in the village of Ter Maaleh for four years now.

I was used to it. My mother wasn't.

She had books, bought in France that were still in their plastic wrappers

← She wore her nightgown all day

The Thorn Birds

She had a 5,000-piece jigsaw and she would spend whole days working on it.

It's Saint-Malo, your family's town.

It'll take me at least a year to finish.

I couldn't understand how anyone could complete a puzzle like that.

You have to start with the edges.

After that, it's easy.

I'm home!

I realized that my parents were growing apart.

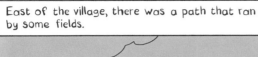
East of the village, there was a path that ran by some fields.

If you followed it, you came to a concrete irrigation canal.

I used to hang out there sometimes with Wael and Mohamed

It took a good 20 minutes to get there

You could see Bedouin tents on the other side

And beyond them, a highway that ran north

Each time my cousins thought about jumping over the canal.

I'm sure I can do it!

Go on, try!

They always decided against it at the last second.

I'll try another time . . . I don't feel like it today . . .

Yeah

I was terrified that they'd try to jump over it and drown

The canal was easily 15 feet wide.

GOD IS GREAT! THERE IS NOTHING GREATER THAN GOD

AH!

It's time to pray.

?

Don't you want to pray with us, Riad?

We can show you how if you want.

I, uh ... I ...

I ... my father told me I could wait a bit longer ...I'll do it later ...

Not ... not now.

They never pressured me into doing it

No problem, Riad!

We'll show you

First, if you don't have a mat, you must clean the ground.

Next, you must wash your neck, your hands, and your feet.

But the canal water is dirty ...

... so if you don't have any water, you can use some clean sand or earth.

You put your shoes behind you ...

... and you work out where Mecca is.

Over there, I reckon.

No one forced my cousins to pray. They did it quite naturally.

The Bedouins were praying, too

31

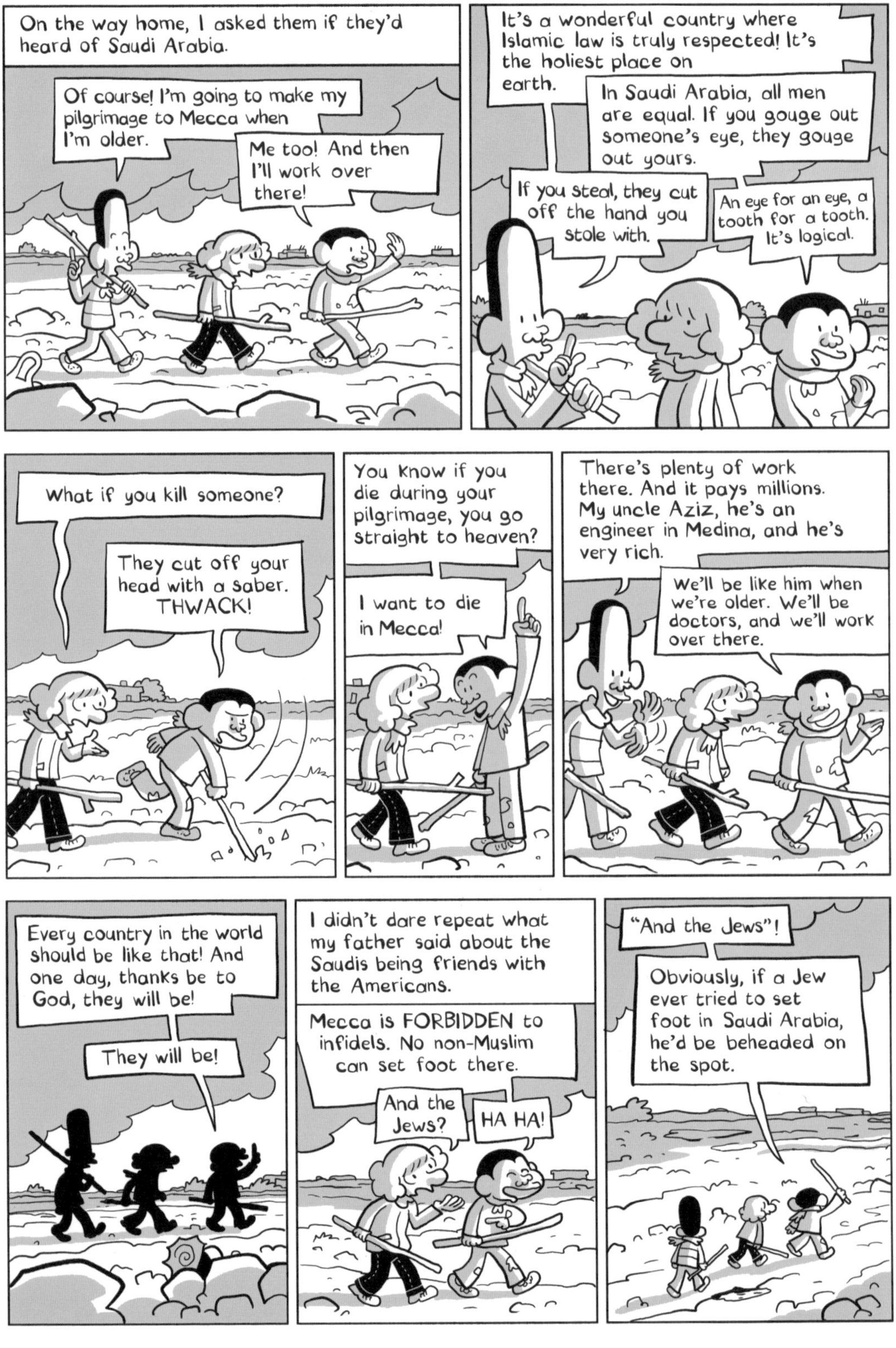
On the way home, I asked them if they'd heard of Saudi Arabia.
Of course! I'm going to make my pilgrimage to Mecca when I'm older.
Me too! And then I'll work over there!
It's a wonderful country where Islamic law is truly respected! It's the holiest place on earth.
In Saudi Arabia, all men are equal. If you gouge out someone's eye, they gouge out yours.
If you steal, they cut off the hand you stole with.
An eye for an eye, a tooth for a tooth. It's logical.
What if you kill someone?
They cut off your head with a saber. THWACK!
You know if you die during your pilgrimage, you go straight to heaven?
I want to die in Mecca!
There's plenty of work there. And it pays millions. My uncle Aziz, he's an engineer in Medina, and he's very rich.
We'll be like him when we're older. We'll be doctors, and we'll work over there.
Every country in the world should be like that! And one day, thanks be to God, they will be!
They will be!
I didn't dare repeat what my father said about the Saudis being friends with the Americans.
Mecca is FORBIDDEN to infidels. No non-Muslim can set foot there.
And the Jews?
HA HA!
"And the Jews"!
Obviously, if a Jew ever tried to set foot in Saudi Arabia, he'd be beheaded on the spot.

Later, up on our roof, I told them about Santa Claus.

A magic man who brings children toys?!?

Yep! You just put a tree in your house and he leaves toys under it.

WHOOAA!

Amazing! And he brings you whatever you want?

Yeah, you have to write him a letter asking for specific things. If you don't, he brings whatever he wants.

WHOOAA

WHOOAA

On Christmas Eve, my cousins decided to try. They found an old branch and stuck it in a brick.

And there's your Christmas tree!

They wrote their letters to Santa.

"We want the same toys as Riad. Even if we only get half of what he gets, we'll be happy."

I put the letter in the brick.

...and tomorrow, you'll have the toys!

AMAZING!

God be praised!

That evening...

My mother had set the table.

She'd made little canapés

My father had managed to find a Christmas tree and some baubles, but he didn't tell us how.

You see, children, this is a Côtes du Rhône, an exceptional wine.

Ah, this really is nice!

MMMMM, delicious!

YUCK! It's corked!

Don't drink it!

What do you mean "don't drink it"? This is a $50 bottle!

I'm going to drink every last drop!

You'd better not, you'll be sick.

It's the perfect temperature. Wonderful!

I think I want to go back and live in France.

In France? What would we do in France?

Have a better life! Yahya will be old enough to go to school soon. I want him to go in France!

The French HATE Arabs!

I'd never find work there.

How do you know? You've never tried!

Oh, I know all about France! France is for the French.

You got your degree at the Sorbonne!

I could never become someone important in France. There are no important Arabs in France. The only place I can make it is here.

What about me? I'd like to be a secretary again! I can work!

My mother is old, and ...

We can see her during the holidays!

FLIGHTS ARE EXPENSIVE!

How do we pay for them?

PFFFFT ...

My trees are finally going to yield fruit this year! I'm going to make my first million!

Mama! Can we go to bed now? That way, it'll be tomorrow sooner and Santa will have come!

The next day, Santa Claus had brought us some fantastic presents.

(In fact it was my grandmother in France who sent the toys)

My father had to pay exorbitant customs duties

I rushed up to the roof to see if my cousins had received their gifts.

The letter was still in the brick

Nothing!

Strange, he brought me lots of different toys!

My cousins were very upset.

Look! The magic man went to Riad's house, but then he forgot us!

I found it hard to understand, too.

All I know is that he doesn't give presents to children who haven't been good.

They went home . . .

. . . and so did I.

My mother was doing her jigsaw . . .

BLECHHH!

. . . and my father was throwing up in the toilet because of the corked wine

We often saw one of my aunts. Her name was Khadija.

She lived in a small house fairly close to ours

I liked her a lot.

The smell of her sweat was very welcoming

SMACK

When she smiled, you had the feeling that everything was fine

She had a kind husband, lots of daughters, and a son of 13 who was always out and about.

They were poor but they invited us all the time

So you get 10/10 at school? Like your father when he was a boy. But that's normal: the son of a genius is bound to be a genius!

What were your grades like at school?

Oh, I didn't go to school ...

I can't read or write.

REALLY?

But Khadija is proof that God is great: she's illiterate but she can read the Quran, and ONLY THE QURAN!

Thanks be to God.

Thanks be to God.

Thanks be to God.

GOD WORKS WONDERS!

No one knows how it's possible! It's a DIVINE MIRACLE!

Oh come on! She learned by reading over your shoulder! She's super smart!

Grrr! You always have to spoil the magic! It was God rewarding her for her piety!

Khadija was one of the few people who asked my father to translate my mother's words.

What did she say?

She said you learned at the same time as me, when I was doing my homework.

NOOOO HA HA!

Khadija was a fantastic cook.

She had a grape vine in her courtyard

She would pick the leaves, wrap them around rice, and stew them.

It seemed completely simple

They smelled of warm rice

The taste was incredibly complex.

Sweet and savory at the same time ... sour and mild

...soft and crunchy

The best way to eat it was to shove the whole thing in your mouth at once

I couldn't understand how these simple leaves could have so many different flavors.

I planted this vine when I got married!

She had a little vegetable garden, and she'd spend hours stuffing her homegrown zucchini with rice and meat. She showed my mother how to do it.

It made them laugh a lot

Of all the people we knew, Khadija was the only one to take my mother's side.

You have a European wife, so why are you living in this hole? You can see perfectly well that she's not happy here!

Yes she is!

Take her back to France! You were lucky enough to have a good education, you got your doctorate in France, and now you've come back to live in this backward place! What was the point of it all?

Her husband stepped in to remind her not to overdo it.

Let them do what they want, Khadija . . .

You act as if you don't have a brain! Go and live in Damascus, at least!

Sniff

What's she saying?

Nothing . . . She doesn't understand . . .

We heard the call of the muezzin.

Everyone went to pray

I went to drink some water

STOP RIAD, STOP!

?

You're a big boy! You mustn't walk past them when they're praying!

Nothing must come between God and the believer! You have to go BEHIND them.

I couldn't understand why my father was so particular about things like that when he wasn't religious.

He watched them pray and smoked

But his eyes looked worried.

Actually, I was thinking that I'm going to observe Ramadan this year!

HUH? Why?

It's good for your health! Fasting purifies the body. It's scientifically proven!

But ...

But I thought you were a liberal? That you wanted to lead the people out of the darkness of ignorance and superstition?

WHAT ABOUT YOU? YOU DON'T BELIEVE IN GOD BUT YOU CELEBRATE CHRISTMAS!

IT'S THE SAME THING!

A few weeks later, we took a path through the village toward the river.

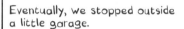
Eventually, we stopped outside a little garage.

I'm going to see where the guy is...

Hello, anyone there? I need to make a phone call!

A tired-looking man appeared and sat next to a box with lots of wires coming out of it.

Where do you want to call? Damascus? Aleppo? Homs?

No, we're expecting a call from France.

Where's that? In Syria?

No, Europe... You gave me your number, so we could receive a call...

Yes, doctor. If the person has the number and they make the call, it'll light up there.

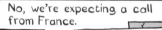

Almost nobody in the village had a telephone. This switchboard had opened very recently.

The man tried to look important

Phone calls were very expensive. My mother had written to my grandmother weeks before to arrange this call, which my grandmother would pay for.

We waited for hours →

Then suddenly, a little red light on the box started to flash.

Hello.

Hello.

He repeated "Hello" a dozen times, then hung up.

CLICK

HFF

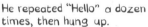

The light came on again.

Hello.

Hello.

Hello.

Um, maybe if ...

SHHHH. Wait, doctor.

Hello.

Hello.

CLICK

I ... um, what happens exactly, when you say "Hello," sir?

Well, someone speaks and I hear "Chabadi chabi" like it's not even Arabic, so I hang up.

We missed our call a few times because of this operator who hung up as soon as he heard a foreign language.

They don't speak Arabic in France? REALLY?

The man forgot this each time, and my father was afraid of annoying him.

Ah! It's ringing!

Hello.

Hello.

Hello.

Psst! That's for us!

Ahhh ... yes.

I should warn you, they don't speak Arabic. You can't understand a word.

My mother began talking to my grandmother and her face lit up.

Yes, Santa came! Everyone was very happy.

The operator started laughing when he heard my mother speaking French.

Our stomach bugs have cleared up.

HFF HFF HFF

No, we're fine now ...

Then, gradually, his face froze as he realized she was speaking a foreign language ...

No more sore throats ...

... and he ended up looking completely baffled.

Riad and Yahya are good ...

My mother seemed even more tired than usual that day.

I don't do much. I look after the children ...

We've got quite a few problems. Life is hard here ...

I said LIFE IS HARD HERE!

And there's something else ...

A catastrophe: I'm pregnant.

I don't know how we're going to cope ...

CHAPTER 2

Conan the Barbarian is a legendary film directed by John Milius.

In the beginning, Conan lives with his parents

They're happy. They are Cimmerians.

His father tells him about life.

Conan is young

Conan's people believe in a god named Crom, who lives on Earth.

Conan has the same haircut as me!

But one day, a horde of barbarians attacks his village.

Conan and his mother find themselves alone in front of the barbarians' chief.

The father is killed! They are the last survivors

The chief takes off his helmet: he is a blue-eyed black man with a very gentle face.

He smiles tenderly and turns away: he has spared Conan and his mother ...

He feels sorry for them!

She lowers her sword, relieved: her son is safe!

But he pivots and, in a single rapid movement, beheads Conan's mother with his sword.

Her head falls to the ground while she still holds her son's hand

Conan looks at his empty hand ...

...then at the barbarian chief.

He narrows his eyes: he'll remember that face

Young Conan is taken as a slave, along with some other children.

They walk a long way.

The music is dramatic!

The children are tied to a wheel, which they have to push endlessly.

Conan turns the wheel. He is regularly whipped. He suffers.

The poor kid is covered in dirt

Years pass and the slave children grow up or die at the wheel.

But Conan keeps going.

His legs are skinny, but he pushes hard

After several years of this, he is transformed: his legs now have huge muscles!

He manages to turn the wheel ON HIS OWN! All the others are dead; he's the sole survivor!

He lifts his head: the little boy has become a Big Strong Man

Conan is bought by a gladiator coach. He fights in an arena and beats all his opponents.

He salutes the crowd who cheer his murders ↙

He is provided with women ...

One night, over dinner, the coach asks his fighters a question.

My friends! We won again. This is good.

BUT WHAT IS BEST IN LIFE?

A sort of Hun with a mustache replies.

The open steppe. A fleet horse. Falcons at your wrist. And the wind in your hair.

arrogant and thinks he knows everything

WRONG! CONAN! WHAT IS BEST IN LIFE?

TO CRUSH YOUR ENEMIES, SEE THEM DRIVEN BEFORE YOU, AND TO HEAR THE LAMENTATION OF THEIR WOMEN.

HOORAY! WHOAH! THAT IS GOOD! YES! THAT IS GOOD.

One night, Conan is freed by his master, for no reason. He just says, GO!

Poor Conan! He runs like crazy! ↙

He is free for the first time ... and he wants vengeance!

49

He takes refuge with a mysterious woman, who seduces him.

She's almost naked, wearing only a skimpy outfit ↓

In fact, she's a witch who transforms into a monster when they make love!

After that, he has lots of adventures and meets a warrior girl named Valeria.

They love each other →

But she is killed by the chief of the barbarians.

So Conan burns the love of his life on a pyre ↓

His friends watch and one of them cries

Why are you crying?

He's Conan, the Cimmerian. He won't cry. So I cry for him.

Finally he tracks down the barbarian chief, who has become a guru for thousands of fanatical followers.

He preaches from the top of a pyramid ↓

Conan enters the building and at last finds himself face to face with the man who killed everyone he loved.

You can tell right away that he's smarter than Conan and has something up his sleeve ↓

My child. You have come to me, MY SON.

HUH?

But Conan is suspicious →

For who now is your father if not me? Who gave you the will to live? I am the wellspring from which you flow. When I am gone, you will have never been. What would your world be without me?

He puts his hand on Conan's shoulder ↓

MY SON.

Conan loses it! This is the only time in the movie when he shows any emotion! He is Overcome ↑

Thankfully, he pulls himself together and beheads the chief of the barbarians in front of the watching crowd.

He looks like he's suffering, and that's good to see ↑

He shows the barbarian's head to the people then throws it down the steps.

It makes a thud when it lands

It was the most incredible thing we had ever seen.

The movie's final image was of Conan as an old man with a beard. He had become king.

From that day on, my cousins and I were transformed into a horde of Cimmerian barbarians.

We made our own weapons of war.

Sheet metal tied to a pole with string

Spear made with sticky tape

Rusted metal bar from a window

We wandered around the village looking for enemies to behead.

We combed the area

CROM!

Over there.

When we saw another group of children, we had to be careful.

We could tell from a distance if the group was peaceful ...

Chatting

Smiling

Younger

... or threatening.

Hunched over

Head up, proud, and fierce. Staring

Mouth open

If they were peaceful, we waved our weapons in their direction and made faces like Conan.

We almost picked a fight with them

GRRR

If they looked threatening, we hid our weapons and looked away.

And if they got aggressive ...

HEY! Give me your sword, son of a dog!

One day, our horde was on its way to secure my father's glorious forest.

The trees had grown a little. This was the year they were supposed to start giving fruit.

There were peach trees and apricot trees.

They were still very small

You could see little fruit here and there, hidden under leaves.

Tiny green peach

There were still a few flowers

This orchard looked so fragile. It was the only one in the area.

Suddenly, in the distance, I saw enemies looking under the leaves.

?

BY CROM!

Anas and Moktar were methodically picking all the fruit off the trees. They ate some and tossed the rest.

I didn't know what to do. I wasn't allowed to fight them. My cousins came to my defense.

Thanks be to God, your father will have no harvest...

My uncles! Stop, that's very bad!

Stealing from thieves isn't theft...

We'll punish you one day for hanging out with that Jew!

I looked at my sword...

I held it tight and hit Anas on the back of his neck as hard as I could.

It really was the best thing in life, crushing my enemy and seeing him die before me.

CRACK

Blood spurted out of him! It was great!

Khh

54

In fact, I didn't do that. We walked away and let them carry on.

You should hit them, Riad. What they're doing is really bad.

They're destroying your father's harvest.

I know, but what if I can't control my strength and I kill them?

You can't kill your own family.

By God, that's true...

Hey, I'm going to take a leak.

Me too!

My cousins always peed standing side by side, totally relaxed. I was slightly ashamed to show my willy. But this time, I decided to act like them.

There was a very pleasant warm breeze

woooooo

Hey, that's funny, your willy's different from ours.

?

Oh yeah, you've got skin there, and we don't!

Huh, strange. Must be a French willy.

We've got Cimmerian willies.

Your willy is completely normal.

It's just that your cousins are circumcised, and you're not.

What's "circumcised"?

It's an operation where they remove the bit of skin at the end of your willy. It's totally pointless ... Muslims do it, but ...

You don't need to ...

How is it possible to remove that?

I'd never noticed that my father's willy was different from mine.

He spent ten or fifteen minutes every day washing his willy under the faucet.

To me, that seemed normal.

Nothing is more important to a man than his willy.

Never let anyone touch it!

You have to take good care of it and always wash it properly, or you might catch all kinds of diseases.

It's easy for your willy to get infected.

SCRATCH SCRATCH

Riad! We have to tell you something!

We found out about French willies with that skin on the end...

Are you sure your mother isn't Jewish?

Of course I'm sure!

She's French.

Because I heard that willies with that skin on the end...

...are JEWISH willies.

My father told me it was normal, that everyone had a willy like that to start with ...

... but then they cut off the end, and that made it into a willy like yours.

Really? I don't remember them cutting mine.

Me neither.

Riad! Maybe your mother is Jewish but she doesn't realize it?!?

Impossible! My father would never marry a Jew.

That's true.

I was really worried about the willy situation. My cousins believed me when I said that Abdel-Razak Sattouf could never have married a Jew.

I have a secret to tell you ...

But would the other children believe me? No one else must ever see my willy!

I'm a Jewish willy ...

Irrigation water wasn't available at that time of year.

How long are we going to have to keep doing this? I'm sick of it!

Until the hot weather comes!

At nightfall, the four of us went to water the trees in the field.

You have to take good care of the trees when they're young.

We all carried bottles of water. My father had a small flashlight to light up our path.

CLICK
CLICK
CLICK CLICK

It didn't work properly and kept going out.

GRRRRR ...

PIECE OF JUNK!

They're over there, look! Straight ahead.

I'm cold!

Don't listen to your mother, Riad, just pour the water near the base of the tree.

Orchards are big business! Everyone loves fruit!

Hee hee!

CLICK!

AHHHH.

My father checked every tree.

He couldn't see any fruit. He looked worried.

He'd stopped blinking

I didn't dare say a word. I looked up at the sky.

I can't see anything with this stupid flashlight!

Oh well, we've watered them. Now we just have to wait for them to grow.

Let's go home.

Look at those stars! The night sky is more beautiful here than in France!

A shooting star! Quick, make a wish!

I wish that we get rich very soon.

Everyone make the same wish! That way, we'll triple our chances.

The Muslim calendar is based on lunar months. It begins in 622, the year Mohamed left Mecca.

The teacher had broken his cane again

So in 1986, it was 1407.

That's a magnificent cane, Riad, but a bit too big for me to hold in one hand!

The lunar year has twelve months.

You! Show me your cane, it looks good.

Hold out your hand.

WHACK

The ninth month is Ramadan.

So? How is it?

He hit him for no reason

RUB RUB RUB

During that month, it is forbidden to eat or drink between sunrise and sunset.

It's good, sir.

Pregnant women, sick people, and children under the age of seven do not have to fast.

Hey! You asleep?

In my class, everyone observed Ramadan.

Riad! Take him out to get some air!

YES, SIR.

Everyone ... except me (but I didn't mention that).

Oh God, I'm so thirsty ...

I ... I have to go back to class.

In the new school, as in the old one, there were no toilets or cafeteria. The children brought their own lunch and ate it in class.

YOU'RE FREE FOR ONE HOUR!

But during Ramadan, they just sat there.

110°F heat.

Each student wanted the others to see him so everyone would know he was fasting.

Some children showed off by spitting so they wouldn't swallow

I said I had to go to the toilet and rushed home to eat lunch.

Take it easy!

Don't have time ...

CHOMP CHOMP

Then I ran back to school and pretended to look desperately hungry.

I had a feeling that no one believed me.

GAAA ... ACH ... COUGH

My father also observed Ramadan. He came home exhausted from the university and collapsed on the couch.

AAGGHH MY GOD

He put on his djellaba with difficulty.

Then he fell asleep reading the Quran.

He stood on the balcony waiting for the sun to set.

Just because it's behind the houses doesn't mean it's set.

Suddenly, a shiver ran through the village ...

...and he rushed to the faucet.

He emptied the entire bottle in one go, straight down his throat without swallowing.

The water poured as if into a bowl

No noise!

And now, time for the barbecue king!

At that moment, a delicious smell of grilled meat began to fill the village.

My father had a very small grill, which he used to cook skewers of ground beef.

He blew on the embers like his life depended on it.

HUFF

FFFF!

I tried to squat in the same position, but my back killed me.

My mother couldn't cook Syrian food, so my father bought prepared food.

There was greasy falafel that smelled of chickpeas and spices

All kinds of kebabs

Fluorescent sodas

The kibbe was delicious. The best moment was when you bit into the center, filled with pine nuts.

Nice salty taste of hot fat

I also adored lahm bi ajin.

It was a sort of pizza covered in sweet and salty meat, which you had to roll up

During Ramadan, lots of people drank a black liquid that tasted of licorice: irq souss.

Mmm, taste this!

YUCK!

It was incredibly bitter and tasted like glue

Black like crude oil

My father drank it straight from the pitcher.

Without making a sound

During Ramadan, he often invited his mother to dinner.

He was proud to show her that he was fasting

Eat! Eat more! You're not eating.

Yes I am...

He was expecting her to praise him. But observing Ramadan was normal for her.

He ate heartily, exaggerating his pleasure.

But you could tell he was disappointed not to be congratulated

My father never asked me to observe Ramadan.

Papa, I was thinking ...

... but I thought it would make him happy if I tried.

I'd like to observe Ramadan!

Oh! GOOD IDEA!

Are you kidding? You're too young!

Everyone in my class does it!

Let him do what he wants!

The secret is to eat in the morning, before sunrise.

Wake me tomorrow!

OKAY, MY SON!

The next day, my father woke me in the middle of the night.

Quick, the sun's going to rise in 30 minutes!

We ate cheese in oil with bread and drank very strong tea.

Fasting is very good for your health. It gets rid of impurities.

Everything the religion recommends is good for your body. Praying calms you, and it's also good exercise. Bending down, leaning forward, getting up again ... it keeps you fit.

Performing ablutions is useful, too: it's hygienic.

STOP!

No more food until sunset!

I went back to bed for a few hours. When I woke up I was already dying of thirst.

You won't make it through the day!

Sure I will.

Walking the three hundred feet from our house to school was exhausting.

Bad breath because brushing your teeth was forbidden ...

In class, my head was spinning.

At one point in the day, the teacher sat down and stopped moving.

Hhh

I thought he was overdoing it.

Ahh ... My God, help me ...

The entire class did nothing until recess.

I felt that I wouldn't survive the day.

My head was as heavy as iron

I was seeing stars.

67

Was it delirium brought on by thirst that made me do what I did next? I had the idea during recess ...

I discreetly went back to the classroom

And I wrote this sentence, taking great care with my handwriting

"The teacher observes Ramadan because he is a good Muslim."

That's what I wrote!

I was proud of myself

The teacher would be delighted

Recess ended. The students returned.

The teacher looked ill.

He read the sentence

Which son of a dog wrote that?

I was so shocked that I put my hand up right away.

My heart had stopped

HOLD OUT YOUR HAND!

WHACK!

I found out later from my father that the teacher was Christian. He pretended to observe Ramadan to avoid trouble.

He'd thought I was mocking him and exposing him publicly.

He was never the same with me

RUB
RUB
RUB

I made it through the school day and managed to walk home.

That day of fasting was the hardest thing I had ever done

YOU HAVEN'T EATEN OR DRUNK ANYTHING? YOU'RE CRAZY!

Nah, it's okay ...

My father came home from the university, exhausted as usual.

So? How did it go?

Fine, thanks be to God.

Riad! Don't say "Fine, thanks be to God" if you didn't stick it out!

But I did!

You look a bit too normal to me ... You must have drunk something!

I didn't!

Pfft ... "Fine, thanks be to God" ...

You should never lie about religion.

No one forced you to observe Ramadan.

What time is it?

VROOM

That was the only time I ever tried to observe Ramadan.

The day after the end of Ramadan is Eid, the festival of breaking of the fast. Along with Christmas, it was my favorite day of the year.

You had to dress nicely and wait on the couch until there was a knock at the door

The men of the family came into our living room.

They sat down, looking at us kindly. Then one of them called my name.

I went over to him.

Smmmack!

Hmmm.

Each man gave me some money.

The poorer ones gave coins

My mother served cakes.

They took them without looking at her

By the end of the morning, I was a rich man!

My father jokingly asked us for the money.

Give me your cash, I'll keep it safe!

NO, it's mine!

Here, Papa! You can have mine!

AHHH!

You're so kind, Yahya! He gave his money to his papa! Now that is a good boy!

Riad is like Hadj Mohamed, HE LOVES MONEY and keeps it for himself ...

He doesn't share.

Yahya is generous, just like me.

I resigned myself to these remarks ...

Because in the end my father kept the money and never gave it back to my brother, who forgot all about it.

SMACK!

My cousins were rich, too. We went to a store made from a container.

All the children went there to buy plastic pistols, firecrackers, and soccer balls.

The firecrackers came in the form of a plastic ring.

The cylinder came out ...

... and you put the ammunition in it

The true specialists took out the mesh stopper from the end of the gun to make flames.

BANG

The village echoed with the sound of firecrackers all day long.

BANG BANG
BANG
BANG BANG
BANG
BANG BANG
BANG

The explosions became less frequent ...

The air had a nice gunpowder smell

BANG
BANG

The festival ended, and life went back to normal.

CHAPTER 3

Sometime later, my grandmother came to visit us with my aunt Khadija.

My grandmother had a permanent grin on her face.

She's asking how the pregnancy's going and if you're in pain.

That's kind. I'm fine.

She says that when she was pregnant with me, I used to move around all the time and kick her, and she couldn't sleep.

Riad was the same!

But this little boy, or girl, is very calm.

A GIRL? NO! I want a boy!

My father translated for his mother. A strange expression appeared on her face.

It will be a boy, thanks be to God! Girls are such a source of worry.

Girls are a catastrophe.

My aunt smiled, too. She didn't take it personally.

Ahhhh yes!

It's true that a boy would be better!

It makes life much easier.

And what about you? Would you prefer a brother or a sister?

A BROTHER!

75

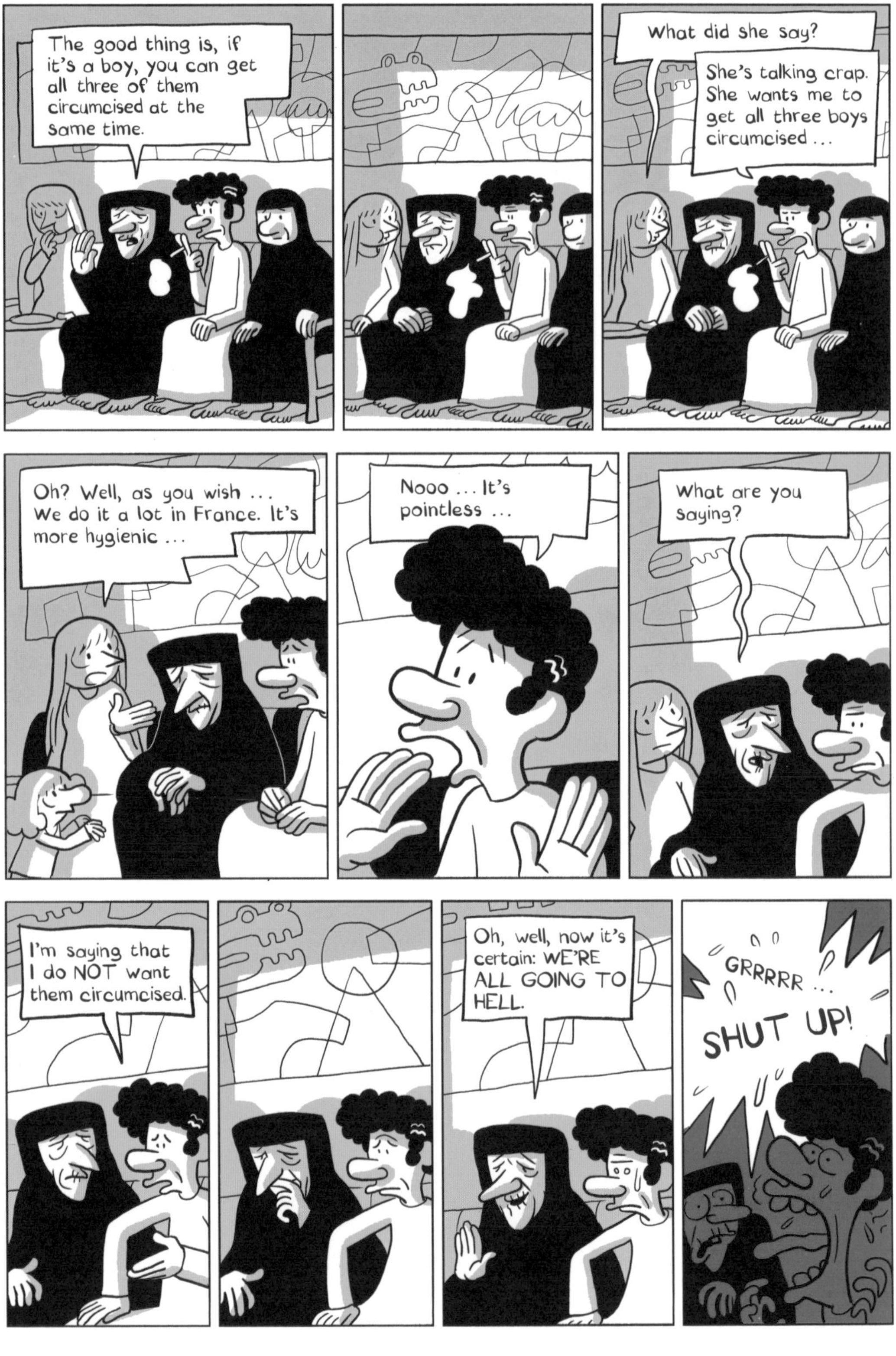
The good thing is, if it's a boy, you can get all three of them circumcised at the same time.
What did she say?
She's talking crap. She wants me to get all three boys circumcised ...
Oh? Well, as you wish ... We do it a lot in France. It's more hygienic ...
Nooo ... It's pointless ...
What are you saying?
I'm saying that I do NOT want them circumcised.
Oh, well, now it's certain: WE'RE ALL GOING TO HELL.
GRRRRR ...
SHUT UP!

YOU RUINED MY LIFE YOU STUPID IGNORANT PEASANT! SHUT UP! SHUT UP!

What did he say?

AAAHH

I don't know!

I CURSE YOUR GOD, YOU HEAR? I CURSE HIM!

DIE! DIE! I DON'T WANT TO SEE YOU ANYMORE!

STOP IT!

HHH

My father continued hurling insults at her for several more minutes.

He was hysterical

He was drooling

Then he ran away.

He left us with his mother, who had fainted.

But why was he so upset?

I don't know!

My mother and my aunt lay my grandmother on the couch.

Oh Lord I'm dyyyyying . . .

I searched the apartment.

Then I heard muttering coming from the balcony.

My God, forgive me for what I said.
My God, forgive me for what I said.
My God, forgive me for what I said.
My God, forgive me for what I said.
My God, forgive me for what I said.
My God, forgive me for what I said.
My God, forgive me for what I said.
My God, forgive me for what I said.
My God, forgive me for what I said.
My God, forgive me for what I said.
My God, forgive me for what I said.
My God, forgive me for what I said.
My God, forgive me for what I said.
My God, forgive me for what I said.
My God, forgive me for what I said.
My God, forgive me for what I said.

CHAPTER 4

I think we have to get up and follow the priest.

Oh?

The air was thick with the smell of incense. The priest sang in a strange language. We circled the room behind him.

My father followed obediently. He looked horribly embarrassed.

The priest came to a halt. The man who had been holding the baby greeted everyone.

Doctor, I admire you for having come to my son's baptism. Thank you.

Not at all, it's normal.

We had finally met my father's very important friend.

Since the row with his mother, my father no longer had any contact with the rest of his family.

You live in a village? Isn't that hard? That's not Syria, you know!

In English

Yes, it's tough.

My mother seemed very happy to finally meet people from beyond the village.

You must travel around Syria! In an hour you can be surrounded by beautiful countryside...

Yes, we're going to buy a car, thanks be to God...

This powerful man was named Tarek and his wife was Sabah. They were very nice.

...and it's true that Ter Maaleh, well...

They lived in a large apartment in Homs.

Crystal chandelier

Not many cracks

They had two daughters who giggled whenever they saw me.

Hee hee

My father refused to tell me what Tarek's job was. All I knew was that he was close to Hafez Al-Assad.

Some wine?

With pleasure.

The Arab world and Syria need modern men like you, doctor.

He seemed to idolize my father.

But I understand your desire to live in your family's village.

All great men are close to their roots.

SLURP

I admired my father's capacity to enjoy life, even after cursing God. There was no worse insult.

He seemed to be coping fine

We've never been to Damascus.

Oh, what a shame! It's the most beautiful place in the world!

I would love to take you to visit the capital.

We can go to Lebanon, too!

Oh, that would be wonderful!

Later in the evening...

Look, Abdel! This is the life I want! Their apartment is great and they have a car ...why don't we have that?

We're working our way up to that level!

JUST BE PATIENT!

But you should have waited for them to offer to take us before you asked them!

I didn't ask them!

Let me deal with them. They're very powerful people...

What do they do?

All in good time.

I'm the politician. I'll handle the negotiations.

Then there was music and the girls started dancing at one end of the room...

AYAYA MY DAAARLING

...and the men at the other.

They looked very serious

DAAARLING AYAYAAA

Shame I'm pregnant. I would have liked to dance, too.

Spring arrived.

Warm, grass-scented breeze

My dying grandmother had survived. We still hadn't seen her again.

You could see her house from our rooftop

My mother had made good progress on her jigsaw.

You could begin to see a city

5000 PUZZLE

My father was more relaxed.

I'm home! Just got back from Damascus!

The exams were in full swing at the university.

I BROUGHT BANANAS!

LOTS!

I still loved bananas

They were expensive and hard to find

My father's students showered him with gifts so he would be lenient when he was grading their work.

Chicken, finely decorated copper bowls, two cacti, a very nice table lamp...

...and even ...A CATFISH!

Can you eat it?

It smelled of mud and dead leaves

Of course! But you have to cook it for a long time. It's very good with tomato sauce.

I loved this time of year.

In the meantime, I'm going to grade these papers.

The top corner of each paper was folded down.

It's so they'll be graded anonymously...

The students did not seem particularly bright.

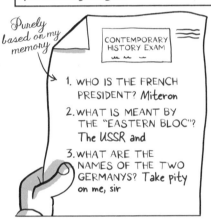

Purely based on my memory

CONTEMPORARY HISTORY EXAM

1. WHO IS THE FRENCH PRESIDENT? *Miteron*

2. WHAT IS MEANT BY THE "EASTERN BLOC"? *The USSR and*

3. WHAT ARE THE NAMES OF THE TWO GERMANYS? *Take pity on me, sir*

The students covered their papers with pleas for leniency. Some of them quoted the Quran or wrote poems.

What do you do to the ones who write in the margins?

It depends. If I can tell they've made an effort to actually answer the question, that's okay.

But if they don't answer it, like this one ...

12. WHO IS THE CURRENT PRESIDENT OF THE USA?

13. HOW WOULD YOU DESCRIBE THE AMERICAN FINANCIAL SYSTEM? (ESSAY)

In the naym of All Mitey God, I beg you for mersy I cudent work this year becos I have a famly of 8 childrun in Deir ez-Z or plese give me a grayd so I can move up to the nekst year or our childrun wi'll starv to death thank you my good teecher by God

HA HA HA

That's what this son of a dog gets!

HISTOIRE CONTE...
0/20 TERRIBLE
1. ~~~~
2. ~~~~
3. ~~~~

I had the impression that it was difficult to corrupt my father.

A few days later, the teacher did not turn up to school.

After an hour, some of the students began to leave the classroom.

He's not coming, thanks be to God. We can go home. We have a free day!

I hesitated for a long time. But after waiting another hour, I stood up.

Riad! You mustn't play hooky! It's the most terrible crime you can commit!

Relax, the teacher isn't coming.

The teacher didn't turn up today! So I came home.

?

I felt guilty for the rest of the day.

STAY, RIAD.

DON'T LEAVE!

PSHOOO

That evening, my cousin Wael knocked on our door.

Riad! Your classmate Saleem told me to tell you that you're in big trouble. The teacher came just after you left, and he sentenced all deserters to the ATLI!

Pure terror

86

It was the worst punishment on earth. "Atli" meant "thrashing." It was a simulated public execution that took place at the end of the school year. I had watched it in the past.

The students stood in rows in the playground

The culprit was tied to a chair

The other guilty ones wept as they waited their turn

The principal read out the nature of the student's crime.

Mohamed REBELLED against his teacher and insulted his parents.

Mercy, sir

A

Another culprit would hold the child's legs as the principal himself delivered the punishment. He hit the soles of the child's feet as hard as he could.

THWACK

From what people said, it was the worst pain ever ...I begged my father to intervene on my behalf.

It was out of the question

My mother insisted. So he ended up going to see the principal, who refused to call off the punishment...

NOPE!

...then finally agreed in return for money.

NEVER PLAY HOOKY AGAIN!

Only pathetic losers skip school.

Think about the other children whose fathers couldn't pay to get them out of it!

This is the last time I pay to save you.

Sometimes my father lifted up the corner of a paper to see a name...

I just don't want to be too hard on one of my favorites.

That's all.

The Lebanese border is about 25 miles from the village of Ter Maaleh, as the crow flies.

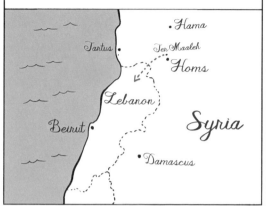

In 1986, civil war was still raging in Lebanon. There were occasional clashes, but it was possible to get there by car.

You want to drive, Riad?

Tarek and his wife took us to explore the region.

Come up here!

There we go!

I'M LETTING GO OF THE WHEEL NOW!

Be careful, Riad! Don't kill us all!

I was really driving!

Look what an excellent driver you are!

You have driving in your blood.

We parked on a bend, overlooking a mountainside.

Come and admire the view...

WHOOOO

We were on the mountain that I could see from the roof of our house!

Suddenly, between two rocks farther down, I saw some narcissus.

The beauty of the flowers, the amazing view, the warm breeze... I felt a weight on my chest.

I had a coughing fit.

I ran over to my mother to give her a flower.

Thank you, darling! Give the others to Sabah!

Thanks! Kiss?

I accidentally turned my head.

She looked to see if anyone had seen, then she blushed.

Thank you for the flowers!

Hee hee!

We got back in the car and drove to Beirut.

Ah, Lebanon! The gangsters run everything here! The Lebanese are the kings of the Arabs because they're corrupt. BUT they are very smart.

The country looked more modern than Syria. The streets were clean.

WHOA!!! Tarek! Let's stop here!

Okay, doctor!

MERCEDES - BENZ

Oh my God!

My father spent a long time looking through the window.

Buy one, it's perfect timing! We'll be free if we have a car!

Buy it, Papa!

Buy it, doctor. I can make sure you won't pay customs duties when we go back to Syria!

He twisted his mouth and rolled his eyes.

MNNNGGG

Everyone awaited his decision.

Okay! We only live once!

DING

DING

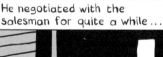

He negotiated with the salesman for quite a while...

...then came out.

It's too expensive and he won't lower the price...I'm going to wait...

The Lebanese are thieves.

As you wish, doctor. Let's get going then.

It was hard to believe that this country had been torn by years of war.

Everything seemed so normal, almost peaceful . . .

All I remember is an enormous military helicopter standing in the middle of some wasteland.

Its rotor blades were like razors ↘

My mother had made friends with Sabah.

It's good to leave the children with their grandparents! I feel like I can breathe . . .

They spoke English together and had no problems understanding each other.

I also took French lessons when I was younger . . .

Really?

France is a GREAT friend of the Middle Eastern Christians. A great friend. It protects them. All the Christians here love France!

"VIVE LA FRANCE!"

You see, Riad, Syria used to be part of the Ottoman Empire (that was the Turks). It was a great empire, but it fell to pieces because it was ruled by idiots . . .

After the First World War, the Europeans divided up the Ottoman Empire (which had been allied with Germany). The English took Mesopotamia, and the French took Syria and Lebanon . . .

The Europeans drew the borders of Syria, Iraq, Kuwait. It was the Sykes-Picot agreement. The Arabs didn't get a choice. The new occupants just took over.

And the French and the English gave power to the minorities in order to protect themselves against the majorities. In Lebanon, the president had to be Christian, the prime minister Sunni, etc. In Syria, it was the Shias who ruled over the Sunnis...

In Iraq, it was the other way around. The majority of the population was Shia, so they put the Sunnis in power.

It was logical. Since all people think they're right, as soon as they have a majority they start killing anyone who doesn't agree with them.

Hee!

You know, Riad, your father is an immense intellectual.

It is an honor for Syria to have him here.

Ooooh, let's not exaggerate.

I mean it.

How many Sunnis from Ter Maaleh would go to a Christian baptism? None. Except you: tolerance itself.

OH! LOOK AT THAT!

A supermarket, like in France!

Oh yes, Lebanon is modern.

It was unbelievable to see such a place here. My mother suggested we go inside.

Why aren't there supermarkets like this in Syria?

There's only one in Lebanon, so let's not exaggerate.

There was hardly anyone inside. The fluorescent ceiling lamps gave only a dim light.

It smelled of bleach and the metal of the shelves

Not as good as France, but still ...if only we had something like this in Ter Maaleh!

The shelves were half-empty

My mother bought detergent, Uncle Ben's rice, camembert cheese, and a few other things. I asked my father if I could go to the toy aisle.

What do you want to do there?

I'm not buying anything!

Just to look!

There was a very small aisle at the back with teddy bears, plastic cars, and a big stack of strange tablets.

They were piled on top of a cardboard box

It was a sort of drawing tablet.

If you drew on it with your finger or something pointy, it left a trace

When you pulled the knob down, the drawing vanished.

It was pure magic

CLACK!

I want this!

NO! DID I BUY THE MERCEDES? NO! SO DO LIKE I DO!

ECONOMIZE!

Put it back.

I'll get it for him, doctor. My pleasure.

Noooo! He's too spoiled.

I insist. It'll be a souvenir of our trip.

There was only one checkout open.

180 pounds, monsieur!

In French

How are you, monsieur? You're French, aren't you?

In Lebanon, everyone speaks French!

PFFT. 180 pounds for nothing... What a waste...

In French

We went back to Syria. Tarek's car was not checked by the customs guards.

The soldiers saluted him affectionately.

Even I felt loved by them!

CLACKT CLACK

LILILI!

I had to know. So I asked Tarek what his job was.

Riaaad! I already told you. Tarek is an important man who works with the president, and that's all.

Tarek winked at me and opened the glove box.

He handed me a photo album.

The album contained badly pasted photos of President Assad. Tarek was behind him in every picture.

Here he was in a stadium ...

... in the street ...

... with some soldiers ...

... with politicians ...

... and even in a car

Tarek protects President Assad. He's the president's bodyguard.

BODYGUARD! WHOOOAA!

Noooo ... It's not just me. There are lots of us who protect him ... We look after the president when he goes out ... to make sure everything is fine ...

What's he like, President Assad? Is he nice? Is he a good Muslim?

Riad ... ha ha ...

HA HA!

HA HA! Of course, he's VERY VERY nice. Like all great men, he has remained very simple. And of course he is a very pious man.

But he respects all religions.

That's why he's the PRESIDENT!

He doesn't really need bodyguards. No one is ever aggressive toward him. Everyone loves him.

In fact, our job mostly involves stopping people who love him too much from getting too close.

People are so desperate to embrace him that you have to tell them no.

That happened to me all the time, too!

I wondered how such a skinny man could be a bodyguard.

He smiled all the time and was barely any taller than my father.

It blew me away to think that I was only one person away from President Assad.

And I was impressed that such an important man was so fascinated by my father.

Only an exceptional man could attract people in the highest positions of power!

AND I WAS HIS SON.

My father never said anything bad about Assad. In fact, he felt inspired by his example.

Damascus looks like the cleanest, tidiest place in Syria

He saw the president as a better student than him...

Damascus! We could live in a nice building like that!

Patience, darling... Patience...

...but believed the two of them to be of the same stamp.

Soon we'll have something better!

We went to visit the Umayyad Mosque...

It was magnificent

Women had to wear veils to enter

...and then the souk.

It was like in Homs, but ten times bigger

I asked my father where the university was.

Oh, it's not near here!

What did your son say, doctor?

He asked where the university is.

YOU'VE NEVER BEEN?

RIAD!

We have to show him the wonderful place where his father works! Come on, doctor!

LET'S GO!

After a 20-minute drive, we stopped outside a modern-looking building.

So this was where my father came every week, dressed in his suit!

It's one of the best universities in the world!

There were no students in the corridors.

It smelled of bleach and cigarettes

The floor was scattered with fresh butts

We passed a white-haired man.

Hello there doctor, how are you?

Hello.

My father acted as if nothing had happened, but I could tell he was annoyed not to have been called "doctor" in return by that guy.

Is he a good doctor?

Nooo, he's crappy and old.

I said hello to him because I'm nice to losers! Remember what I told you!

It's a nice university, isn't it?

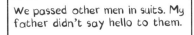

We passed other men in suits. My father didn't say hello to them.

We're not going to spend all day here, are we? We've seen it. The lecture halls are closed.

Did they wear djellabas at home, too?

Tarek was delighted.

The future of the Arab world is growing within these walls.

Suddenly, my mother felt dizzy.

You should sit down for a while.

Let's go to my office.

We went back the way we'd come. So we had gone past his office and he hadn't shown it to us!

Smell
of stale
tobacco

I'm fine,
I'm fine.

I couldn't believe it. His office was dirty and smelled bad. My father acted as if nothing was wrong.

It's very small, Papa!

Who cares! I never come here, and I share it with someone else.

Suddenly, the door opened. The white-haired doctor we'd seen earlier entered the office. He took an envelope from a drawer and left.

Anyway, Riad, I'm your father's student this year. And by God, it's been the best year of studies I've ever had.

I hope to pass my exams with flying colors!

I dream of being a doctor, too.

So now I understood that his invitation to the baptism, his kindness, and this trip were bribes. My father admitted later that Tarek only went to the university one other time: the day of the exam. He wrote his name and my father's name on his paper and left the rest blank.

CHAPTER 5

Come on! It's time to go to school!

We were back in France for the birth of the baby, which was imminent.

We were staying with my grandmother

The teacher is very nice, you'll see. She said that if you had any learning gaps, she'd give you extra instruction.

HA HA

Loser! Ha ha!

Smell of mass-produced hot chocolate

There's only one class, with all the grades in it. That makes it easy for her to put you in a lower grade if you're not at the same level.

There's no grade low enough for your retard son.

My father had stayed in Syria. It was October and the new college semester was starting.

We're going to beat you up!

Charles will take you there.

I was going straight into third grade. What would happen?

I went to school like you, you know ... It wasn't called third grade back then ...

Charles, my grandmother's boyfriend, was a very nice man.

I was your age in ... hang on ... 1923! My God ... Time flies.

I was going to school because mother had decided to spend the first three months of the baby's life in Brittany.

The teacher came to meet me at the gate.

Hello, Riad, I'm Mrs. Loiseau, your teacher.

I was fascinated by her wrinkly skin and the absence of a chin.

Her eyes looked tiny behind her glasses

I stood in the playground and didn't move.

The children all had lace-up shoes and book bags. They didn't wear smocks, and their clothes were clean and brightly colored.

We went into the class-room without singing the national anthem.

Some girls giggled and stared at me.

I put on my Conan face

106

The classroom was well lit. The floor was made of wood. The air had a reassuring smell of wax and dust. The walls were decorated with maps and children's drawings.

Riad, come sit up front!

You're the only one in third grade!

The teacher introduced me saying that I came from Syria.

As you can see, Syria is a Mediterranean country.

It's supposed to be very beautiful, and it's located in a region named?

Anyone know?

The Middle East!

Very good.

Some fourth-grade students started whispering.

Yaouenn! Gurvan! PLEASE TRY LISTEN-ING!

SHE DIDN'T CANE THEM! Her stern voice was enough.

The teacher gave me some exercise books, textbooks, and pencils. It was all free!

The textbook looked very old

The class was divided into four grades.

The big ones looked pretty nice and welcoming.

The little ones seemed more fearful.

The teacher wrote sentences on the blackboard and asked the students to take turns reading them out.

Le peuuu ... tiiit ... chhh ... iiii ... en ... est ...

Le petit

French school is easy!

When it came to my turn, I read the sentences perfectly.

You read like a fifth grader!

I did a few French and math tests. I knew all the answers.

Your mother's done a great job! I'm very impressed.

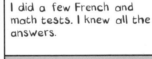

I felt like an exceptional being

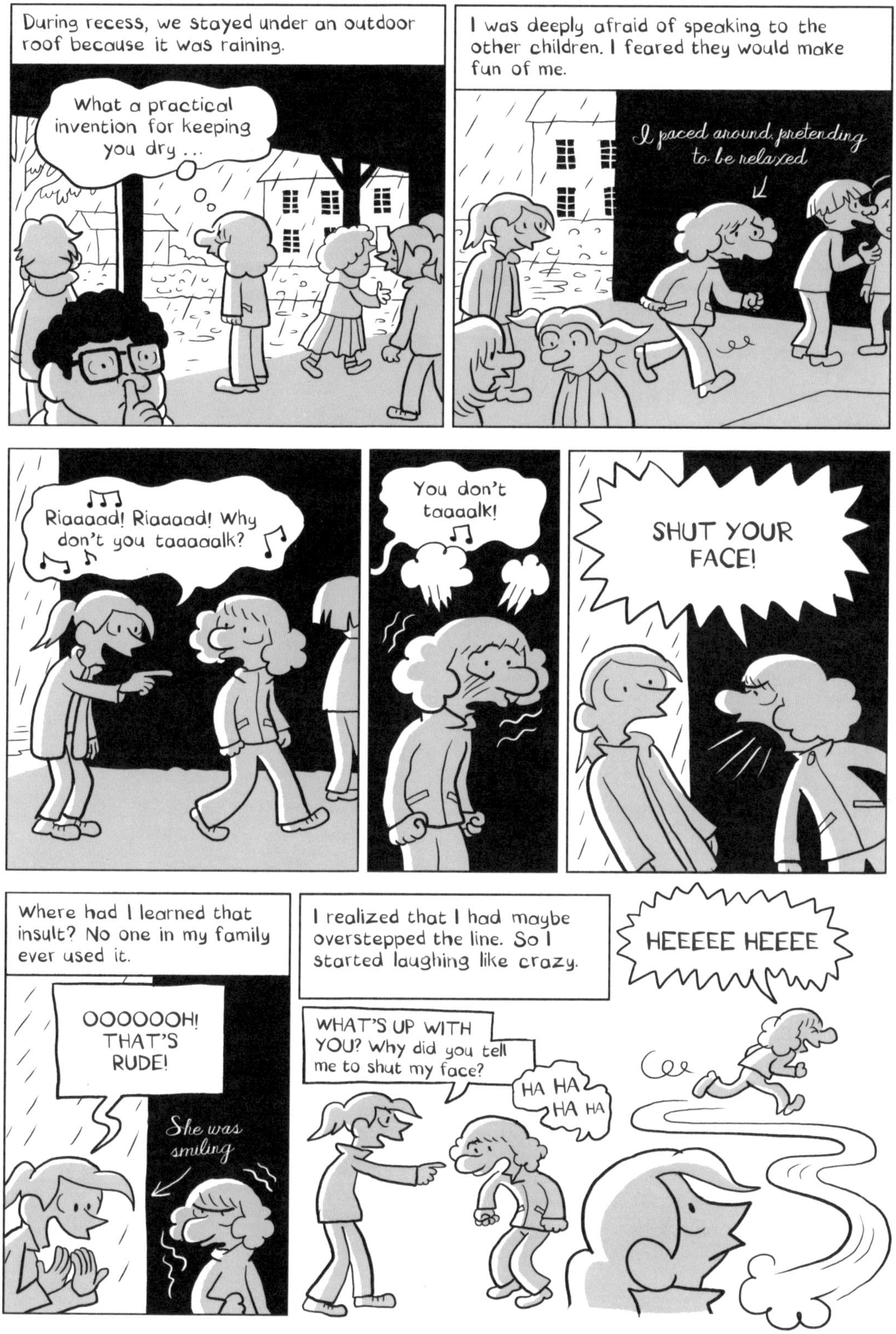

During recess, we stayed under an outdoor roof because it was raining.
What a practical invention for keeping you dry . . .
I was deeply afraid of speaking to the other children. I feared they would make fun of me.
I paced around, pretending to be relaxed
Riaaaad! Riaaaad! Why don't you taaaaalk?
You don't taaaalk!
SHUT YOUR FACE!
Where had I learned that insult? No one in my family ever used it.
OOOOOOH! THAT'S RUDE!
She was smiling
I realized that I had maybe overstepped the line. So I started laughing like crazy.
HEEEEE HEEEE
WHAT'S UP WITH YOU? Why did you tell me to shut my face?
HA HA HA HA

At noon, the students ate in the cafeteria. It was a sort of restaurant for children. I only went there once.

People dressed in white put the food directly on our plates

There were mashed potatoes that smelled like steam.

It had no taste

And a sort of yellow cube with a damp crust, also tasteless.

This was "breaded fish"

The other children seemed to like it. Some even asked for more yellow cubes.

But this girl ate nothing and just stared at her plate

Next, there was vanilla yoghurt and a clementine.

The yogurt was like a sweeter version of labne (very nice)

After lunch, we went to the big kids' playground.

Our teacher walked around with the first-grade teacher, deep in discussion.

Our teacher lived in a little house that was part of the school.

She had a parrot

Sometimes the door opened and a very elderly woman came out.

She looked like our teacher, but much older

It took her ten minutes to cross the playground and go into the street.

That's the teacher's mama! They live together!

She's a bit scary.

There was a massive tree near the wall.

It had lifted up the asphalt around it

The ground was covered in leafy seeds.

Look!

It's a helicopter!

The boys played soccer, just like in Syria. But the atmosphere was less aggressive. No girls were allowed.

I got out of breath easily. And as soon as I started running, I wanted to pee.

PASS IT!

The girls played hopscotch...

...or jumped rope.

Their movements were very graceful.

You want to try?

Yeah!

It was a revelation! I became one of the girls.

When the other boys saw me jumping rope, they became interested, too.

Miss, we'd like jump ropes, too!

Really? Okay.

It became a sort of competition.

22! 23! 24! 25! ...

I was pretty good.

47! 48! 49! 50!

Even the teacher had a go.

But the only game that really united the girls and boys was dodgeball.

GO ON, RIAD, SMASH THEM!

Two teams took turns throwing the ball. If the ball hit you and you didn't catch it, you were out.

YEEEEAAAH!

With many of the kids, there was a lag time between the moment they saw the ball hurtling toward them ...

...and the moment when they ordered their muscles to duck it.

BLAM!

But I managed to dodge all the balls.

I was always the last survivor on my team

The students never talked about God or religion at school.

The teacher didn't talk about politics either

The wind

There were no Muslims in the village.

School ended at 4:30 p.m. every day.

The parents' cars were parked outside

If the class went on a little too long, some parents would honk their horns.

This made the teacher sad

HONK HONK HOOONK!

Friday was the end of the week for me.

Are you going to catechism tomorrow morning?

No, what's that?

It's where you learn about the Bible and all about the Lord...

It's in another school, where the pastor is. He tells us about Adam and Eve and all that, it's REALLY GOOD.

Even if the pastor is very strict, because if we ever mess around he says that Jesus is going to die again and again and it will all be our fault.

And he's already dead, Jesus...So we don't mess around because we don't want to kill him again by being bad.

I didn't understand any of this

We never phoned my father, and he didn't call us, because it was too expensive.

I didn't miss him at all.

Would you like a saucisson sandwich, Riad?

Oh, sure!

In fact, I was even pretty glad he wasn't there, and that made me feel a bit guilty.

crunch crunch crunch

I drew lots of scenes of barbarism.

I enjoyed the savagery.

Whoa! That's violent! It's good though.

It's VERY WELL DRAWN.

YES, VERY.

I really liked receiving compliments for my drawings.

It was my main motivation, in fact.

How could a family like ours have produced such a talented artist?

It's a MYSTERY.

She was genuinely puzzled by this!

My mother spent all day in her chair, talking with my grandmother.

I didn't want any more children, and then this happened!

Oh! But babies are the best!

Yes, but it's so hard, life in Syria ... It's like the Middle Ages.

How am I going to cope with three kids?

Then come back and live in France!

Yes, that's what we're going to do. Abdel has changed. He realizes we can't go on like this.

He doesn't get along with his family anymore ... We'll come back to France and I'll find a job.

You've told me that before! But every time, it's one more year, then another year, and another ...

At that rate, I'll be dead and you'll still be in that village ...

Ha ha, but this time it's for real ...

After the birth, we'll go back to Syria to finish the school year ...

... and then Abdel will look for a job in France.

Sometime later, my grandfather came to visit us with his new girlfriend.

Hello, comrade!

It was the first time my grandfather and Charles had met

I found it hard to believe that he and my grandmother could ever have been married.

Your grandfather told me you liked animals, so I brought you this book on reptiles.

We just got back from Bora Bora, what a place!

LE MONDE des REPTILES

They were so different.

Bora Bora? I'd find it strange swimming in a warm sea . . . I like the English Channel.

Brittany is pretty, but I need sunshine!

I have to be naked in the sun.

Eventually, everyone started talking about my father and our life in Syria.

Ah! You're coming home! What wonderful news! Riad and Yahya are so thin!

Their faces grew serious.

He was such a brilliant student! Why does he want to waste his time in these third-world countries?

He's just had a very bad fruit harvest . . . This time we'll definitely be coming home!

LE MONDE DES REPTI...

Definitely . . . Definitely

I hope so.

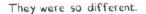

My grandfather loathed religion.

Listen carefully, children! BEWARE people who ask you to "believe" in someone or something.

If you watch them carefully, you'll see it's THEIR interests that you start to believe in... not yours!

Religion is the true scourge of humanity!

My mother was a medium. She made tables shake.

SHE COULD SPEAK TO THE DEAD.

It's true! I saw it with my own eyes!

And she always said, "Heaven and hell don't exist. I know because THE DEAD TOLD ME SO!"

"There is something after death, but it must remain SECRET." She never told me what there was! My poor mama, she was such a kind woman.

LE MONDE DES REPTILES

After the restaurant, my grandfather and his girlfriend returned to their hotel, and we went back to Cap Fréhel.

I asked my grandmother if she believed in God.

Pff, no. Your grandfather hated priests and wanted them all hanged, so we never went to church.

But I did have you baptized in SECRET!

REALLY? I NEVER KNEW!

Well, it's true.

It's so strange, knowing that I was baptized...

It was because of the priest.

What's a priest?

They're men who aren't allowed to be with women and who love Jesus.

Your father would have killed me if he'd found out!

He doesn't know?

OF COURSE NOT!

One day, when you were a baby, I went for a walk in the village and I saw the priest, all in black...

He spotted me and said, "I've never seen you in church with your baby." And I said, "No, we're not believers..."

"Oh really? And do you know what happens to children who die without being baptized?"

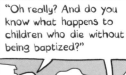

N-No?

"THEY END UP ALONE IN THE VOID!"

"Baptize your daughter! AND SHE WILL BE SAVED!"

I was so scared! I couldn't let my daughter end up alone in the void!

So, I went to church and the priest gave you a quick baptism.

You never know... If God does exist, you're covered.

After working in Paris, my grandmother had returned to retire in the place where she grew up, Cap Fréhel.

There were lots of farmers living there.

The tractors were more modern than the ones in Syria. My grandmother knew everyone.

That's Koulmig, Fanchon's son. He's a nice boy. He looks after his parents' farm on his own.

You see those things on either side of the tractor? They're for spreading fertilizer and pesticide, to protect the crops.

It's very hard to be a farmer! Koulmig went to agricultural school. You have to be very good at science.

Let's go and say hello to Fanchon. She hasn't seen you since you were born!

That's her farm over there!

We came to her door.

BAM!, BAM!

FANCHON?

She's deaf.

FANCHON! YOU THERE?

BAM! BAM! BAM!

Well look who it is—Bondious!

How's things? Is Jeannot here?

Oh yeah!

It smelled of manure and sweat

Boh!

Ooh Bondious, what cute littluns!

Aren't they cute?

Ha, oh yeah, they're cute all right!

Who wants cookies?

Fanchon and my grandmother chatted. I found it hard to understand what they were saying.

So Miss Clementine's back? S'good! And Mr. Abdel?

Ha, still over there.

My grandmother spoke with the local accent

There's Gurvan, who's at school with you. Ain't you spoke with him? He's my grandson!

Yes!

Oh yeah, he works good.

Jeannot did not participate. He stared at the tiles.

HH...

Sniff.

HHH

HH

Kh! Kh!

He looked exhausted

We chatted for a while and then took the little path back to the house.

Fanchon and I used to play together when we were little!

We went through the gate at the bottom of the garden

The lawn was soaking wet.

There's an underground spring, but it's not always active.

PLOTCH PLOTCH

Come on! Snack time!

The secret is to stuff lots of camembert inside and butter both pieces of bread.

Fat is EXCELLENT for children.

Here.

DING DONG

?

Huh? It's Fanchon!

122

Hey! I forgot earlier, but my cat had littluns! D'you want one?

Look at the cute 'lil kitty cats, Riad!

Four kittens were wriggling inside the bag.

Oh Grandma, can we have one?

Looks like he's a cat lover!

No thanks, Fanchon! I prefer dogs!

Meow

I've never really known what to do with cats!

It don't matter none!

Meow

My grandmother went back to the kitchen. I watched Fanchon leave.

She walked past the dumpster, then came back and put the bag on top of it.

BANG! BANG! BANG! BANG!

The bag was still moving a little bit

I went to tell my grandmother.

Grrrr! If she's going to kill her cats, she should put them in her own trashcan!

I'm going to give them back, she can't have gone far ...

All done! That Fanchon, she's nice but what a yokel.

Her husband, Jeannot, was a hunter. He doesn't hunt anymore because he's too old, but he used to take his rifle everywhere to shoot rabbits.

He had lots of dogs that went hunting with him. They'd fetch the prey after he shot it.

He loved those dogs.

Well, when one of them got too old, he tied it to his cart and used it for target practice.

Dogs he'd had for ten years! I saw it with my own eyes.

But that was nothing. When he realized that his hands trembled and he couldn't hold a rifle straight anymore...

...Well, he shot all his dogs at point-blank range. After that he had them cut up and he sold his rifle.

I said, "Why'd you do that to your dogs? I thought you loved them..." And you know what he said to me?

"Bah! I couldn't hunt no more. What was I going to do with them?"

Sometime later, there was a huge storm in Cap Fréhel.

WOooo o Ooooo Oo

The roof creaked and branches tapped on the shutters.

WOOOO

CRRAKK! TK!

My brother was sleeping. The power was out.

WOOOOoo

CRak! FRRR!
cúci, cúci

My mother wasn't in her bed. I got up.

WOooooOoooo

WOOOOOoowoOOOOOO

The wind knocked down a power line!

It's coming, I can feel it! Charles is going to take me to the hospital in Saint-Brieuc ... Be a good boy!

Saint-Brieuc is nearly thirty miles from Cap Fréhel!

I always dreamed of being a race-car driver, so I'm not scared of a storm!

They left.

I stayed with my grandmother. We had a hot lemon drink.

WOOOO°O°O°OOO°OO

VRcHK

TSSSSTING

RAK

TcHK

TicTic TicTic

I'm terrified of storms! You know what happened to me, when I was your age?

WOOOOoo

TcKRR

There was a bed over there.

CRKK

I slept there with my mother. One night there was a storm, like this one. The thunder boomed and the lightning flashed.

BROO°°°

VRRRR

Mama was asleep, but I was awake.

CRA K

I had the feeling that something STRANGE was going to happen!

KSSSS

Suddenly, the wind died down and the thunder fell silent.

WO°°°°°°°

Mama started speaking Breton in her sleep . . .

Emaa tont or sideri jenn...

AND A GREAT LIGHT APPEARED!

A BALL OF FIRE CAME DOWN THE CHIMNEY AND INTO THE HOUSE!

It spun around and made a weird sound. I'll never forget it.

I woke Mama and she started to cross herself!

The ball flew around the room three times . . .

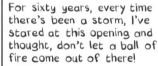

. . . and then it went back up the chimney.

This chimney.

For sixty years, every time there's been a storm, I've stared at this opening and thought, don't let a ball of fire come out of there!

I hope the birth goes well and they don't die in an accident!

The next morning, I woke up early and went down to the living room.

VROOOOM VROOOOM

Hi, Riad! Sleep well? Everything went fine last night, you have another little brother! He's very cute.

Apparently he's very blond and has even more hair than you.

We drove to Saint-Brieuc.

It was very sunny when we got to the hospital.

Inside, there was a smell I'd never smelled before: cleanliness and death.

The smell was everywhere, all the time!

We went into a small room. My mother was in bed reading *Paris Match*.

Your brother's in the little crib over there. His name is Fadi!

Yahya and I went over to him.

SATOUF
FADI

He started crying and we saw
something amazing.

A tooth!

AHHH!

Funny, isn't it? He was
born with a tooth! Like
Napoleon and Alexander
the Great! Apparently
it's the sign of a great
future!

And me?
Was I born
with a
tooth, too?

Oh no! Not you
or Yahya! Just
FADI!

CHAPTER 6

Three months later, we returned to Syria. My father had prepared a surprise for us.

The family had come to meet us at the airport!

YOOYOOYOOYOO YOOYOOYOOYOO!

My father had hired a minibus.

That mustache! Ugh!

I know! It's just to make you laugh!

He had made up with his mother.

What a handsome boy he is, with his tooth!

She looked very happy.

Smack

I have several pieces of very good news, but I'm not going to tell you them all right away!

Life is going to be MUCH better in the next few months!

And boys...

...We're going to get all three of you circumcised! Happy? You'll have the same willy as your papa!

During our absence, my grandmother had forgiven my father, who immediately made a few concessions. Circumcision was one of them.

We arrived at night. There was no electricity in the village

Did you see my new flashlight? Look, it works! That's one of the pieces of good news that I wanted to tell you!

HA HA HA! JUST KIDDING! HA HA HA!

There was the noise of a motor...

VROOM VROOM

...AND THE LIGHTS CAME ON!

We have a generator now!

We can watch TV even when the power's out!

GREAT!

VROOM VROOM

At bedtime, I asked my father what exactly happened during a circumcision.

You see that bit of skin? The circumciser cuts it off, and then it's all over!

SNIP!

That must really hurt!

NOOOOOO! It stings a little, but that's all! You hardly feel it!

Good night, son!

When I pinched the end of the skin with my fingernail, it really hurt.

My brother was oblivious to everything.

Once you're circumcised, you'll be a man, like papa! It's a VERY IMPORTANT OCCASION!

You can choose a gift, and I'll get it for you!

Yes ... because it does hurt a little bit, in fact.

Ha ha

Ahem

All right ... You can have that Grandizer as your circumcision present.

YES!

It's good to be happy. We believers are all circumcised. It's a tradition and traditions must be respected. We believers are all a big family and nothing is more important than family.

Without family, we're nothing.

We did some shopping in Homs, then took the bus back to the village.

When will you buy the Grandizer?

I'll come back! It'll still be there. Who would pay that much for a toy?

Except me...

Look! It's good old Tamer! How are you, my brother?

H...Hello, father of Riad...

We sat down in front of Tamer, my father's old school friend. He was scared of snakes and afraid my father would make hissing noises and humiliate him in front of the other passengers.

Hey, Tamer...Would you like to hear my son recite the first sura of the Quran?

Go on, Riad.

I did it. Tamer listened to me, fascinated.

How wonderful, by God! A blond-haired boy with a French mother, and yet he's so pious!

But tell me, Riad, do you prefer your father or your mother?

Uh, well... my mother.

OH! ...I'm getting off here!

WHAT THE...? WHY DID YOU SAY THAT?

I dunno.

Even if it's true, you should have lied and said my father!

Syrian boys always prefer their father!

Grrrr! What are people going to say?

"My mother wah wah wah"

Only girls and babies prefer their mother...

We got off the bus. My father walked ahead of me.

Sniff

I could see that for him, it was time I became a man.

That night, I dreamed I was in a labyrinth . . .

Two bulls were charging at me . . .

. . . but a giant hand picked me up and saved me at the last second.

It was Grandizer.

SORRY, BY GOD. I HAVE TO TAKE IT FROM YOU.

My willy was in his other hand!

BOOM
BOOM
BOOM
BOOM
BOOM
BOOM
BOOM
BOOM

It was still there

Weeks passed. The day of my circumcision drew closer, but I tried not to think about it.

The donkey that our neighbors used to throw rocks at was dead. Its body had been left near the river.

We always took a detour to look at it. We were fascinated by its slowly rotting corpse.

One day, I threw a rock at it to see what would happen

It stuck to its skull

I am still slightly ashamed that I did that, even now

Yuck!

My cousins were very happy I was going to be circumcised. That meant I was definitely not a Jew.

I bet the Cimmerians are circumcised.

Yeah, I think so, too.

I asked them about the operation.

We don't remember it, we were too young... But maybe circumcision is like Conan's wheel of pain. It hurts, but once it's over, you're a real man.

The only thing that reassured me was the huge cardboard box in the storeroom cupboard.

The Grandizer

But my father caught me looking at it.

What are you doing here?

I'm looking at my circumcision present!

What are you talking about? That's my RIFLE!

Hee

Tarek, my bodyguard student, got me a license. We'll go hunting this summer!

The barrels are side by side, the way I like it!

Listen, when I went back, someone had already bought it!

Never mind!

You're a man now. You don't need toys!

By the way, not a word to mama about the rifle! She'd kill me if she found out I paid $3,000 for it!

141

The day of the circumcision arrived.

The living room was full of all the important men in the family. Their faces were grave but sympathetic, as if to say, "It's going to be unpleasant, but look, we all got through it."

I didn't know all of them →

There was a knock at the door. Everyone thought it was the circumciser.

Tarek! Thank you for coming!

Of course.

We had to wait another two hours.

I have an idea! Why don't we NOT circumcise me?

HA HA, don't talk nonsense.

KNOCK KNOCK

I put on my Conan face.

The circumciser was like an older Syrian version of Arnold Schwarzenegger!

This guy's job was to cut the ends off willies all day long →

As was customary, he told a joke so we would forgive his lateness.

A Bedouin goes to an electrical-goods store in Homs to buy a TV. He stands in front of the one he likes and says, "This TV looks good, how much is it?" The salesman says, "You're a Bedouin, aren't you?" and the guy says, "Amazing! How did you know that?" and the salesman says, "Because it's not a TV, it's a fridge."

HA HA HA HA HA HA HA HA

Next, four men surrounded me and my father walked away.

He had a strange look on his face.

He left the room...

My aunt Khadija's husband blindfolded me and held my arms. The circumciser opened his leather bag.

He'd put a handkerchief on the floor →

The blindfold slipped just as the circumciser cut me.

Oops

This is what I saw.

It hurt a lot. My gaze alighted on Tarek.

My mother told me later that my father locked himself in the storeroom and wept while it happened.

My brothers were circumcised, too, but I don't remember that because I fainted.

When I woke up, there was a huge bandage around my willy.

It took a few months to heal, because the circumciser's razor was not very clean.

We'll have to cut the whole thing off! Ha ha, no, I'm just kidding . . .

The doctor

I had to stay home for a while.

I walked like a cowboy

I explained to my father that I was glad I'd been circumcised because now people would stop saying I was Jewish.

Huh? What are you talking about?

Jews are circumcised, too!

I didn't dare tell my cousins that. Anyway, they stopped talking about circumcision . . .

. . . and they didn't want to talk about *Conan the Barbarian* either.

That movie you made us watch is forbidden by God, Riad! It shows naked people!

We must never speak of it again!

I never found out what caused this U-turn.

My mother had been very upset by the circumcision. For her, this was the final straw.

Thankfully, my brothers healed more quickly than me →

One night, my father came back from the university...

...IN AN EXCELLENT MOOD!

This was the moment she chose.

We have to talk! I've had enough. I don't want to live here anymore. I want us to go back to France. I want a nice apartment, supermarkets, good schools...

TIME TO LEAVE SYRIA!

My God! It's a sign!

What?

I AGREE WITH YOU!

We have to leave! I can't stand it either!

REALLY?

YES! I'm sick of this corrupt country where you can't do anything! TIME TO LEAVE SYRIA!

Listen, while you were in France, I applied to a few PRESTIGIOUS UNIVERSITIES!

NO!?! REALLY?

And on the very day you say this to me, I received THIS! IT'S DESTINY! IT WAS MEANT TO BE! IT'S "MEKTOUB," AS WE SAY!

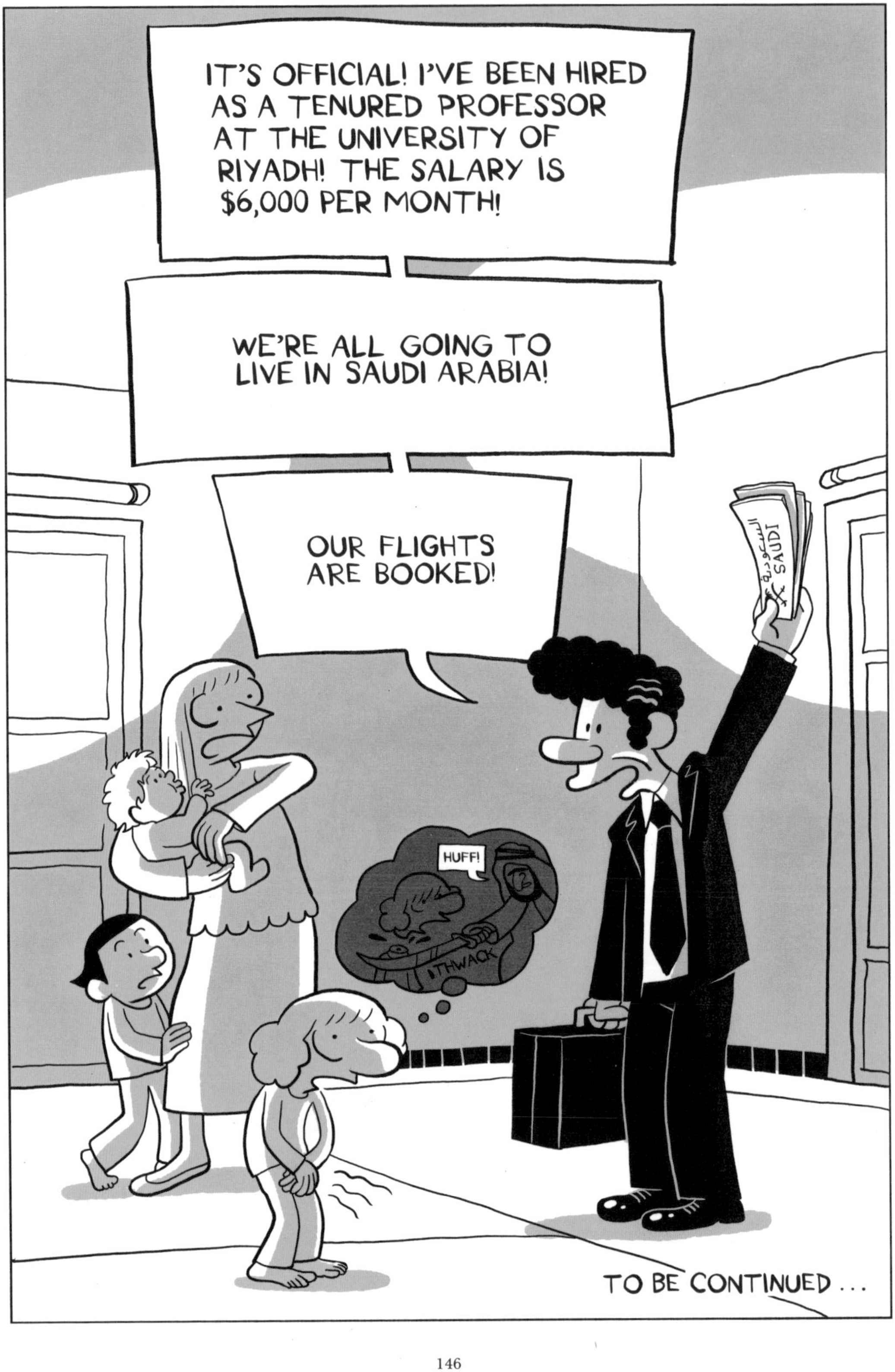
IT'S OFFICIAL! I'VE BEEN HIRED AS A TENURED PROFESSOR AT THE UNIVERSITY OF RIYADH! THE SALARY IS $6,000 PER MONTH!
WE'RE ALL GOING TO LIVE IN SAUDI ARABIA!
OUR FLIGHTS ARE BOOKED!
SAUDI
HUFF!
THWACK
TO BE CONTINUED . . .

ABOUT THE AUTHOR

RIAD SATTOUF is the author of the bestselling *Arab of the Future* series, which has been translated into twenty languages. For the first volume, he received the Angoulême Prize for Best Graphic Novel and the *Los Angeles Times* Book Prize. He grew up in Syria and Libya and now lives in Paris. A former contributor to the satirical publication *Charlie Hebdo*, Sattouf is now a weekly columnist for *L'Obs*. He has also written three other comics series in France and directed the films *The French Kissers* and *Jacky in the Women's Kingdom*.